MY CITY
MY FAMILY
MY HISTORY

MY CITY
MY FAMLY
MY HISTORY

John Malia

Elephant Memoirs

This book is a work of non-fiction based on the life, experiences and
recollections of the author. In some limited cases names of people,
places, dates, sequences or the detail of events have been changed solely
to protect the privacy of others. The author has stated to the publishers
that, except in such minor respects not affecting the substantial accuracy
of the work, the contents of this book are true.

Although every precaution has been taken in the preparation of this book,
the publisher and author assume no responsibility for errors or omissions.
Neither is any liability assumed for damages resulting from the use of
information contained herein.

Printed on FSC accredited paper.

*Cover photo: the author's father, John Malia, in 1942, adapted from a
photo of Durham Cathedral from Palace Green*

To my mam, Biddy, for making me laugh

To Aunty Margaret,
for looking after the family archives

CONTENTS

INTRODUCTION

My name is John Malia. I have been researching my family tree for a number of years now. I decided to start writing these stories in 2020, the year the world was having a crisis which will no doubt become part of our own history, the coronavirus! I continued writing through to August 2021.

The first section of my book contains a brief history of Durham City.

In the second section of the book, I talk about my grandad and his three brothers, the first generation of the Malia family born in England. Their father, old James Malia was an Irish immigrant, born around 1854 in County Longford, Ireland. It has not been possible to get his exact date of birth, as it was slightly different for him on the census records. Around this time, Ireland was suffering the effects of the Potato Famine. This was a time of great hardship in Ireland when the potato crops had blight and many families were starving and penniless. James decided to try his luck in England and came over in the early 1870s. At this time, many Irishmen came to work in England in manual jobs, such as mining, building and farming.

Old James Malia married and had four sons who were all born in Durham City: oldest to youngest, James, Thomas, John, and Joseph Patrick Malia, all of whom joined up and fought in the First World War. James Malia, the eldest son, was born in 1877 and was my grandad.

In the third section I write about my father's generation.

In the fourth section, I finish with my own life story.

These stories come from documents, and the living descendants of old James Malia. I would like to thank each individual for their contributions

I have written these stories for several reasons. I want them to be passed on to my grandchildren and anyone else in the family; I want family members that have died in the world wars to never be forgotten for the sacrifices they made during this time; and I would like there to be a permanent record of our family, the Malias.

The custodian of our family records was always my Aunty Margaret. It was she who handed on to me the postcards, photos, medals, and a box of letters. When I started writing this book, I always sent her each story, so she was the first person to read them. 'They're lovely, our John,' she used to say. Sadly, she wasn't able to see the finished version of this book as she died in the coronavirus pandemic in 2020. She had a stroke and was sent from the hospital to a care home, where she died a week later.

When readers finish these stories, I hope they'll feel they know my ancestors, like I now do. They're not just names. They were people.

Generations of Malias in this book

OLD JAMES MALIA 1851

CHILDREN OF OLD JAMES MALIA
James (Senior) 1877, Michael 1879,
Thomas (Senior) 1880, Catherine 1884,
Michael and Martin 1886, **John (Senior)
1888,** Margaret 1891, **Joseph Patrick
(Senior) 1895**

CHILDREN OF JAMES MALIA (Senior)
James (Junior) 1909, Allan 1911, Mary
1914, Joseph Patrick (Junior) 1917, **John
(Junior) 1919,** Thomas 1921, Laura 1924,
Kitty 1928, Margaret 1931

CHILDREN OF JOHN MALIA (Junior)
Joseph Patrick 1948, Bridget Mary 1949,
Veronica Theresa 1950, Bernadette 1953,
John Malia (Author) 1956, Denise 1958

CHILDREN OF JOHN MALIA (AUTHOR)
Benjamin 1978, Matthew 1982

THE HISTORY OF DURHAM CITY

FROM THE BIRTH OF THE CITY TO THE PRESENT DAY

Durham City from Framwellgate in the nineteenth century

W̲e know that a settlement existed in Durham City during the Roman occupation of Britain. The remains of Roman buildings were found near Old Durham Farm around 1939 by a local man, while quarrying for sand. Old Durham, or Auld Duresme as it had been known in Norman times, had a Roman road called Cade's Road. It is said by several historians that most Roman remains in the Durham City area were lost by quarrying of sand there.

TENTH CENTURY

We could say, however, that the origins of Durham city date back to St Cuthbert, a shepherd boy from the borders who eventually became the Bishop of Lindisfarne. The monastery of Lindisfarne was founded around 634 AD by an Irish monk, St Aidan. It became an important monastery in Celtic Christianity and this is where Cuthbert died and was buried.

Cuthbert's body was later exhumed when the Vikings invaded from the North East. His body, still intact, was taken by the monks who settled first in Chester Le Street. It was said that while they were looking for a safe place to rest St Cuthbert, one of them, named Eadmer, had a vision of St Cuthbert asking them to take him to a place called Dunholm.

On their journey, the monks met a milkmaid who was looking for her dun cow, which had been seen at Dunholm. The milkmaid showed them the way there and eventually the monks reached Dun Holm or 'hill on an island'. This was a raised piece of land surrounded by the River Wear. This story is immortalised on the north wall of the cathedral, in the eighteenth century carving of the milkmaid and her cow.

In 995 the monks built a wooden minster called the White Church and here St Cuthbert's remains were laid to rest. In 999 a new white church was built in stone, and this became the shrine of St Cuthbert.

ELEVENTH CENTURY

In 1006 the Scots, under King Malcolm, were defeated at Durham City, and the captured Scottish heads were displayed around the city walls as a warning to others who wanted to attack. By 1018 the Bishops of Durham had established the County of Durham. In 1027 King Canute visited Durham, walking barefoot to visit St Cuthbert's shrine. The Scots would invade one more time in 1038.

In 1066, after the Normans invaded Britain, William the Conqueror decided to take control of Durham. He wanted to see St Cuthbert's body to find out if it was preserved; if it was not, he would kill all Durham senior churchmen. Legend has it that before the King saw the coffin, he became breathless, panic-stricken and feverish, and thought there must be a strange force protecting St Cuthbert. William immediately fled on his horse and did not stop until he was near York, where he thought he was outside the limits of St Cuthbert's powers.

In January 1069, King William sent a force of seven hundred men to storm the city. The Durham people and a large part of the Northumberland army slaughtered the Normans around the narrow streets of Durham. During this time, the monks fled to protect St Cuthbert's coffin and body, and did not return until 1070. King William was not happy about this and sent an even greater army to burn and plunder the land between York and Durham, to force the people of the North to accept Norman rule.

A castle was built in 1072 by the Normans, who thought this would control the people of Durham. In 1083 a Benedictine priory was formed to help the monks protecting St Cuthbert's body. The Bishop of Durham was becoming more and more powerful and in 1091 William II (grandson of William the Conqueror) granted the Bishop royal powers. This included the title of Prince Bishop, which meant he was given powers to raise an army, create barons, mint coins and levy taxes. These powers and his title were kept until around 1836 when they were abolished.

In 1093 they started to build the cathedral. The original building took around forty years to complete and was much smaller than the building as we see it now.

TWELFTH CENTURY

In 1104 St Cuthbert's body was laid to rest in the cathedral, although this was not completed until 1133.

In 1120, Framwellgate Bridge was built across the River Wear, and the boroughs of Framwellgate and Milburngate were formed. In 1160 Elvet Bridge was built, later repaired in 1225. Elvet Bridge had a chapel on each end, showing what an important landmark it was. Both these bridges had traffic going across them up until around the 1980s, but today they are both pedestrianised. Further boroughs were formed: St Giles, which grew around St Giles' Hospital, was built around 1112, and the Borough of Elvet was formed around the same time. These boroughs were on the main route to the North and this area became home to wealthy merchants and artisans.

At this time, there were mills used for grinding flour, and also cleaning and thickening wool. The main industry at this time in Durham was leather tanning.

Bishop Flambard, when in residence in the castle, looked out on the palace green where there were several buildings. He decided that these buildings and their residents could be a danger to the church from fire and pollution, so he had them all cleared out. Once this was done, grass was laid and the rule, according to local legend, was that the only people who could go on the grass were residents from the castle, to play croquet. Apparently, the rule still stands today, but no one enforces it.

THIRTEENTH CENTURY

In 1237 the monks started building Finchale Priory, on the outskirts of Durham City next to the banks of the River Wear. The building was finished around 1277 and had four monks in residence at any one time, on a four-weekly rotation from Durham Cathedral. The rules were relaxed here for the monks, and it was probably seen as a holiday retreat for them! Later, during the reign of Henry VIII and the dissolution of the monasteries, Finchale Priory fell into ruin and remains a small tourist attraction.

FOURTEENTH CENTURY

There was a murder on Framwellgate Bridge in 1318. The Bishop of Durham's steward, Richard Fitzmarmaduke, was killed by his cousin Ralph Neville (both wealthy and powerful men in Durham) after a long-standing quarrel between them. The first town hall was built in 1356, and also the Almoner's School.

FIFTEENTH CENTURY

During the fifteenth century, two more schools were opened on Palace Green, one teaching music and the other grammar. Today the university still has a music school there. At the north end of the city two hospitals were built, one dedicated to St Mary Magdalene, and a leper hospital dedicated to St Leonard.

There were two prisons in Durham at this time. The one under Elvet Bridge was called Old Bridwell House, or the House of Correction. The other was the county gaol, owned by the Bishop of Durham and rebuilt early on in this century on Saddler Street. Framwellgate Bridge was also rebuilt after a flood destroyed the old bridge around 1400.

SIXTEENTH CENTURY

At this time, Durham, like many towns and cities around the country, was struck by an outbreak of the plague. It struck Durham several times between 1544 and 1598. During this century, Henry VIII sent his men to destroy the shrine of St Cuthbert. This caused a dent in Durham's finances as fewer pilgrims came to visit it. Henry VIII also removed some of the bishop's powers, but the latter still retained the title of Prince Bishop and still controlled Durham. The bishop formed a corporation of a mayor and alderman, who carried no powers.

There were gallows in Durham at Dryburn, close to the site where University Hospital of North Durham now stands. One of the famous people who was hanged there was the Catholic priest John Boste, for practising the Catholic faith. He was hung and beheaded in July 1594. In 1970 he was made a martyr by Pope Paul VI.

SEVENTEENTH CENTURY

When the Civil War broke out between King Charles I and parliament, the Scots took the side of the King and in 1644 they once again occupied Durham. Cromwell's men won the battle, and four thousand Scottish prisoners were taken and held in Durham Castle. Framwellgate and Milburngate became more populated and wealthy merchants and artisans started moving out.

EIGHTEENTH CENTURY

Durham's population was steadily growing. It rose to about five thousand, and early on in this century a mustard industry started up. In 1718 the Blue Coat charity school opened. In 1722 the first theatre opened on Saddler Street, and apparently the actors used to meet in the Shakespeare pub, a place that is still going today. In 1771 Elvet Bridge was damaged by a large flood, and in 1790 an Act of Parliament was passed that set up for a body of men to pave and light the streets with oil lamps.

NINETEENTH CENTURY

This was probably the century of fastest growth for Durham. The population in 1801 was seven and a half thousand, and expanding fast. The organ factory in Durham was becoming famous. There was also a carpet factory.

Because of the Industrial Revolution, which had relatively passed Durham by, there became a greater need for coal, of which Durham had lots. Mines were opened around Durham County with a number of collieries within the city's boundaries. The collieries were Kepier Colliery in 1818, Framwellgate Moor Colliery in 1838, Houghall Colliery in 1841, Keiper Grange Colliery in 1844, Cocken Drift Mine in 1847, Elvet Colliery in 1858, Dryburn Grange Colliery in 1860, Durham Crook Hall Colliery in 1873 and finally Aykley Heads Colliery in 1880. These collieries were no more than two miles from the city centre. In Durham County there were many more, some of which kept going until the 1990s.

As coal mining started to increase, labour was brought over from Ireland, mostly Catholics who established themselves in the Framwellgate, Milburngate and the Elvet areas of the city. Over this time, these areas developed into slums and became problematic. Because of the needs of the Catholic Irish in Durham, two Roman Catholic churches were built. St Cuthbert's RC Church in Elvet borough was built in 1827, two years before the Catholic Emancipation Act of 1829. St Godric's RC Church was built in Framwellgate borough in 1864.

By the mid-1800s the population of Durham had grown to fourteen thousand, and continued growing. In 1832 at the start of Queen Victoria's reign, the Prince Bishop of Durham lost all his powers under the Great Reform Act, apart from keeping his title.

During this century, Durham was moving with the times. Durham Prison was built in 1820, the city was lit by gas lighting in 1824 and in 1832 Durham University was established. Durham had a police force, formed in 1836.

The railway reached Durham in 1844 via Leamside, just outside the city, and in 1857 the railway was brought into the heart of Durham by means of a viaduct at the top of North Road in the city centre, and the building of Durham Railway Station at the north end of the viaduct. Durham County Hospital at the top of North Road was opened in 1860. It was eventually turned into a mental health hospital towards the end of the twentieth century but was closed in 2010. It has now been converted into student accommodation for the university.

In 1834 the government passed the Poor Law Amendment Act. It meant if anyone was poor, destitute or homeless, they should report to the local police station and get a ticket to go to the workhouse at Crossgate. Conditions there were poor and most of the people were treated like prisoners, forced to work long hours and given only basic food.

Looking at a census for 1881, the Durham Workhouse had 153 residents. The youngest was Hannah Marsh, aged one year old. The oldest person in there was Ann Laydon, aged ninety-one years old, with an occupation of labourer. The occupations ranged from scholar to skilled workers, tailors and cabinet makers. Also, there was a section for handicapped people. In this section there was one blind person, six 'imbeciles' and one 'lunatic'. Most of the buildings are still there today, a reminder of the dark past, one now an old people's home.

Because of the growth of the coal mining industry and the start of the miners' union, the first miners' gala took place in Durham City in 1871. Locally it is known as the Big Meeting, and is still going today, even though there are no mines left in Durham County. It has always been a popular event. At times there were up to two hundred thousand people attending the event. Although 2020 and 2021 were cancelled because of the coronavirus pandemic, it is hoped the Big Meeting will continue once we are over this. The only other times it has been cancelled during its one-hundred-and-fifty-year history were during the two world wars, and the strikes in 1921, 1922 and 1926.

TWENTIETH CENTURY

By the beginning of the twentieth century, the population of Durham had grown to around twenty thousand and was still growing. Coal mining production peaked, producing 270 million tons in 1913. In 1923 there were around 170,000 miners employed in the industry. During both world wars, like most men in the country, miners volunteered to join up. From what old soldiers have told me, they reasoned that 'it was safer fighting a war than being down the mine.' A lot of the miners joined the Durham Light Infantry and apparently during World War One some of them were used, because of their mining skills, to dig tunnels under enemy lines to plant and detonate explosives.

The university expanded, creating several new colleges

and also building science laboratories in South Road.

In the 1920s, the slum areas of Framwellgate, Milburngate and Elvet had major problems and it was decided that they would be pulled down. A new estate was built on Sherburn Road about one-and-half miles outside the city centre to house the people who lived in these slums. At the start of the 1930s the estate was completed, and the people moved into their new homes.

Dryburn Emergency Hospital was opened in 1940 at the north end of Durham. After the war it became the main hospital in the city and was known as Dryburn Hospital. On the same site, a new hospital was built and opened in 1998. In 2001 the hospital became a teaching hospital and was renamed University Hospital of North Durham. Some small sections of the old Dryburn Hospital still stand on the site and are still in use.

During World War Two, Germany had a Nazi propaganda broadcaster nicknamed Lord Haw-Haw. Durham locals, including my mother, told the story of one of his broadcasts, which always started with the announcement 'Germany Calling, Germany Calling'. On one particular day, he talked about Durham and 'the beautiful banks of the River Wear and your nice little city and your magnificent cathedral'. Then he said, 'We are going to bomb your cathedral tomorrow and raze it to the ground.'

The next day a thick mist came over Durham all day. Although people heard the drone of planes, they thought the Germans couldn't get a fix on the cathedral and dropped their bombs elsewhere. How true that story is I don't know, but maybe it was the spirit of St Cuthbert protecting the city.

Maybe the Germans were just like William the Conqueror who fled Durham thinking St Cuthbert had magical powers when he tried to discredit the story of the body being intact.

Lord Haw-Haw was William Joyce, an Irish American born in Brooklyn, New York. He was educated in England, yet he was a fascist who at the start of the war fled to Germany and became a propaganda broadcaster. After the war, he was convicted of high treason and hanged on 3 January 1946.

After World War Two, things changed throughout the world; working conditions improved and people had more money, better working hours, and more leisure time. In Durham it was no different. People bought houses, cars and went on holiday.

At this time the population of the city started to grow again, and more private housing was needed to meet the demand. The narrow roads of the city centre were becoming gridlocked due to the increase in traffic. Something needed to be done. New private housing estates were built from the 1960s onwards including Belmont, Cheveley Park, Gilesgate Moor, Crescent Estate and Newton Hall Estate (which at the time was the biggest private housing estate in Europe). By-passes were built to route the flow of traffic away from the city centre. Included in these bypasses were two new roads and two new bridges, Milburngate Bridge, opened around 1968, and New Elvet Bridge, opened in 1975, plus a pedestrian bridge across the River Wear.

In 1963 a new county hall was built, housing most of the county's administrative departments, at the north end of the city near Dryburn Hospital. The county council was one of the city's and county's largest employers.

By the end of this century, Durham and the university had grown steadily. The population of the city and suburbs was around sixty thousand, with a student population of around fourteen thousand. Jobs and new industries continued to grow.

TWENTY-FIRST CENTURY

Durham continues to expand and change as new buildings replace the old. Not all the people who live in Durham agree with the changes; some believe the character of the city may be in danger of being lost.

One of the changes made in 2002 was the introduction of a congestion charge for vehicles going up to the Peninsula from the marketplace. It was the first place in the country to have a congestion charge, which caused a lot of problems for vehicles. There was a rising bollard on entering the marketplace and a charge of two pounds was made to go up to the Peninsula. Once the money was paid, the bollard would sink into the road. On numerous occasions, drivers tried to avoid paying or, due to malfunctions, the bollard rose when vehicles were moved over it, thereby damaging them. The bollard was removed soon after its introduction due to ongoing problems.

This has been a brief look at the history of the city where I was born, over its first twelve centuries. I hope you have enjoyed it. I just wonder what will happen in the next few centuries.

Carving of the monks carrying St Cuthbert's coffin into Durham

The milkmaid carving on an outside wall of the cathedral

The Shakespeare pub in 2021

FIRST GENERATION
OF THE
MALIA FAMILY

JAMES MALIA (Senior)
Born 2 October 1877

James Malia (Senior)

James Malia (Senior) was born on 2 October 1877, a year after Alexander Graham Bell patented the telephone in 1876. Queen Victoria had been on the throne for forty years, and reigned for another twenty-four years before her death in 1901. Twenty-six years later, the Wright brothers successfully flew the first aeroplane in 1903.

EARLY YEARS

When he was born, James's parents lived at 13 Framwellgate, Durham city. Old James Malia was born around 1851 in County Longford, Ireland, and his mother was Mary Ann (formerly Prendergast). They met in Durham and the story goes that when she first saw him, she thought he was from the Mediterranean because he was so tanned and handsome. They were married in 1876 at St Godric's Roman Catholic Church, in Durham City. A year later their first son James was born and baptised there. The family lived at 28 Milburngate, Durham City.

At the time James Malia (Senior) was born, there was no compulsory schooling for children. When James was three, the Elementary Education Act of 1880 was introduced, and school attendance became mandatory for all children from the age of five until they were ten years old. This act was the result of a build-up of several acts of parliament over the years to help protect young children in the workplace. Can you imagine having to leave school at the age of ten to start work? James, however, still had eleven years to wait before he could have a vote in the elections. At the time that James left school at the age of ten, the retirement age was seventy, which meant a long lifetime of working.

James Malia (Senior) was the eldest of nine children and had six brothers (three of whom died at the age of three months old) and two sisters. Their names were, Michael (died as an infant), Thomas (Senior), Catherine, Michael and Martin (twins, died as infants), John Malia (Senior), Margaret, and Joseph Patrick (Senior).

The family lived at several addresses in Durham city centre, including (1891 census) 13 Framwellgate and (1901 census) 62 South Street.

James worked in several jobs after he left school at the age of ten, including pit sinker. This was a hard and dangerous job as the men had to dig a mine shaft by hand. In fact, it was one of the most dangerous jobs in the mining industry at the time. He then worked as a coal filler at the gas works, a soldier, and as a corporation worker.

BOER WAR

Towards the end of the nineteenth century, the British army was fighting the descendants of Dutch settlers – the Boers – in modern-day South Africa, mainly over control of the rich diamond deposits recently found in the region.

In 1899, at the age of around twenty-two, James Malia (Senior) joined the Durham Light Infantry 4th Battalion (service number 5786), and served in the Second Boer War in South Africa until 1902, when he was awarded the Queen Victoria South African clasp and medal at the Orange River.

On 21 February 1904, his mother Mary Ann (Prendergast) Malia, died of cardiac failure.

On 30 August 1908, James was enlisted into the Durham Light Infantry 3rd Battalion Special Reserve Regiment, as he had already gained some fighting experience. He joined the regiment (service number 7694) as a private and was demobbed on 17 April 1912 from this battalion.

MARRIED LIFE

James Malia (Senior) got married at the age of thirty-one to Mary Emma Fowler (born 1887) in Sunderland. They were married on 12 December 1908 in Durham City. On 4 August 1909, his first son was born at Framwellgate, Durham City, and was named James Malia (Junior). The 1911 census shows that James Malia (Senior) was married and lived with his wife Mary E (Fowler), his son James and his father old James Malia at 71 Framwellgate. On 17 June 1911, Allan, his second son, was born at Framwellgate, Durham City.

FIRST WORLD WAR

After being called up by Queen Victoria for the Boer War, James Malia (Senior) got the call from King George V, to fight in World War One.

At the start of the war, James joined Durham Light Infantry 2nd Battalion (service number 10249) as a private. He was thirty-seven by then.

On 7 October 1914, his eldest daughter, Mary, was born. During the war James and his wife and their children sent postcards to each other. They were written in a very formal way, often starting with Dear Wife, Dear Husband, Dear Son and Dear Daughter. This was normal for that time; a small selection is shown in this story.

A typical soldier's diet during the First World War on the front line was a breakfast of tea, bacon and bread. The dinner in the middle of the day was meat and vegetable pressed beef stew, potatoes and porridge. Later on, there would be a tea of cold meat, bread, jam and tea. This diet was probably a lot better than what the people back home were having at the time.

There was one thing soldiers had to do every day on the front and that was to shave, although they had to grow a moustache if they could and were encouraged to keep it. (That's probably why when you look back at photos of first world war soldiers, a lot of them have a moustache.) On 11 February 1916, James' father, old James Malia, died of a cerebral haemorrhage at the age of fifty-seven.

On 1 July 1916, James Malia (Senior) also lost his brother John Malia (Senior), at the age of only twenty-eight. He was killed in action at the Battle of the Somme, serving as a private with the Durham Light Infantry 15th Battalion (service number 15365). James was allowed home this year and, on 27 April 1917, his third son was born and was named Joseph Patrick after the boy's uncle who was away, fighting in France.

Sadly, on 23 June 1917 Uncle Joseph Patrick was killed in action while serving with Durham Light Infantry 2nd Battalion (service number 11769). He was only aged twenty-two. When Joseph Patrick had first arrived in France to join the battalion, he managed to meet up with James (Senior), his older brother. Before he enlisted, Joseph Patrick had been living with an aunt, Margaret Prendergast, in Easington,

County Durham. Her married name was Clark. When Joseph Patrick joined up, he was recorded as Joseph Clark. When James (Senior) found this out, while in France, they both went to the company sergeant to get Joseph Patrick's surname corrected. Sadly, before this was done, Joseph was killed in action.

James (Senior) was transferred to the Labour Corps (service number 21290) and was discharged 22 November 1918 aged forty-one. He also had another brother, Thomas (Senior), who served during the war with the Engineers and Waterways Corp. At some point, after an injury, Thomas was transferred to the Agricultural Corps and was discharged in 1919. By the end of the war, James Malia (Senior) had lost two brothers and his father, but had gained a daughter and a son.

BACK HOME AFTER THE WAR

On 29 December 1919, James Malia's fourth son, John Malia (Junior) was born. After the war, James worked at the gas works in Framwellgate, Waterside, Durham City, as a coal filler. He was made redundant in 1927 when modern machinery was brought in to do this manual work. According to the 1920 and 1930 electoral registers, James and his wife and children lived at 83 Framwellgate, Durham City.

On 21 December 1921, James Malia's son Thomas was born. On 7 July 1924 his second daughter, Laura, was born. On 17 February 1928 his third daughter, Kitty was born and 17 July 1931 his fourth daughter, Margaret, was born.

In 1933 James Malia (Senior) had weddings to go to

because his oldest son James Malia (Junior) married Mary Bell, and his oldest daughter Mary married Christopher J Grant.

FINAL HOME

In the early 1920s Framwellgate and Milburngate were seen as slum areas; they were damp and dilapidated, and had outside toilets that froze up in the winter. Tin baths were kept outside and were brought in for bath nights to be filled with hot water boiled in kettles and pans.

So new housing estates were built on the outskirts of the city centre and the houses of Framwellgate and Milburngate were demolished in the 1920s and 1930s. James Malia (Senior) and his family moved out of Framwellgate, to Maple Avenue on a new housing development called Sherburn Road Estate. According to the 1939 register, James Malia (Senior) and his wife Mary Emma and seven of their children were all registered at this address.

The family's new home had running hot water, an inside bathroom, gas and electricity, four bedrooms, and gardens back and front. What a luxury compared to where they came from! All that for about seven shillings (worth about £24 today) for a week's rent.

When World War Two broke out, James heard the call from another monarch, King George VI, for men and women to join up and serve their country.

James applied to join up once again, but he was turned down by the Ministry of Defence, who suggested he join the Home Guard. He refused, wanting to be amongst the fighting.

At the beginning of the Second World War, emergency laws made it compulsory for lights to be out during the night. The penalty for breaking this was a fine. James broke the rules and was taken to court. The story was reported in a local newspaper in December 1939. James said he was tending his youngest daughter, Margaret, who was ill at the time with tonsillitis. The court fined him five shillings, to which he replied, 'You'll get it when Nelson gets his eye back.' The fine was promptly paid by his wife Mary Emma.

During the war, two of James's sons and one of his daughters joined the services. Joseph Patrick was in the Royal Artillery but sadly was wounded and captured and died in the hands of the enemy on 6 June 1942, aged twenty-five. John Malia (Junior) joined the Royal Engineers for the duration of the war and was demobbed in 1946 aged twenty-seven. Laura (Malia) now Ditchburn, served in the WAAF for the duration of the war and was demobbed after the end of the war.

CHILDREN'S WEDDINGS

Laura married Jacky Ditchburn in 1945 and had a daughter Mary but sadly Laura died in February 1950 when her daughter was only two years old. James (Senior) and his wife Mary Emma brought up Laura's baby daughter Mary until she was an adult.

Between the 1930s and 1950s James Malia (Senior) had at least sixteen grandchildren and several great-grandchildren.

The next of his children to get married was John Malia (Junior), who married Bridget Casey, and Thomas, who married Martha Waller, both in 1947. The last two to get married in 1952 were Kitty, who married Ronnie Barker, and Margaret, who married John R Friend. Allan never married.

THE FINAL YEARS OF JAMES MALIA (SENIOR)

A neighbour remembers James when he moved into Maple Avenue and said that James dug over the large front garden and planted it full of potato seeds. In the back garden he planted other vegetables. While a lot of people on the estate made lawns or filled the gardens with flowers, James was intent on feeding his family.

In the 1950s, some of his grandchildren remember, James had a friend called Mr Oliver who he used to visit at his bungalow (now demolished) near New Durham Club. They also remember on Sunday afternoons when they were about five years old, they would sit at the window waiting for a wave from their grandad as he passed their house on his way to the George and Dragon pub. James was always smartly dressed and they said they never saw him drunk. On Sundays he used to have a drink in the Rising Sun pub and then would finish in the George and Dragon on Sherburn Road Estate. He also liked to play pitch and toss on Rabbit Hill, a local name for fields behind Sherburn Road bottom estate.

Pitch and toss was an illegal game played by throwing two coins in the air and betting if they would both land on heads. (In Australia the game is called two-up and their troops used to play this game in the trenches in 1914. When Australians celebrate Anzac Day in the servicemen's clubs, they are allowed to play the game only on this day, in memory of their soldiers who died and fought in World War One.)

Also in the 1950s, James had a crossbreed dog called Peter. The story is that the dog used to walk down to Claypath in Durham City by itself and hop on the bus back up to Sherburn Road. Apparently, the bus drivers knew it was James's dog and didn't mind giving it a ride back.

During his lifetime, James had served for both Queen Victoria and country, and King George V and country. He had also been a son, brother, husband, father, grandad and uncle. He was born and lived in Durham City all his life, apart from military service. He had worked from the age of ten for fifty-five years, retiring around 1942 at the age of sixty-five.

JAMES'S DEATH

Sadly, after being married for fifty-two years, James Malia (Senior) died on 4 April 1960 aged eighty-two. He passed away at his home at 23 Maple Avenue. At the time of his death, James had sixteen grandchildren and four great-grandchildren. He is buried at St Giles Church, Gilesgate, Durham City. James's wife Mary Emma died thirteen years later in 1973, at the age of eighty-five. By then she had moved to 36 Maple Avenue.

During his life James had seen six monarchs on the throne, the invention of the telephone, then the television, the first flight of an aeroplane (by the Wright brothers), education for all children (Education Act 1880), two world wars, mains gas and electricity installed in most homes, and decent housing provided for the masses.

James's oldest daughter Mary Malia, born 7 October 1914

James's wife Mary with their children, James, Allan, Mary, and the baby Joseph Patrick, taken during World War One. This was probably the first time James saw his new baby son

Milburngate Waterside gas works showing the gas cylinder and the old ice rink

GOD BLESS DADDY AT THE WAR (1).

When the shades of night are falling, oft I dream that I am there,
With my little baby kneeling by the side of Daddy's chair;
Though her prayers are " God bless Daddy ! " not one whisper reaches m
But I know while she is praying what her prayers are sure to be :
" God bless Daddy at the war ! "
Daddy knows, and God is near, " God bless Daddy ! " I can hear ;
What those lips are praying for is " God bless Daddy at the war ! "

A selection of postcards James and his family sent to each other during the war (originals held by Durham County Records Office)

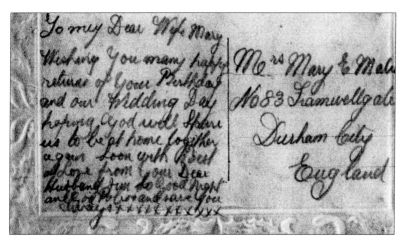

James (front row, second from right shovel in hand, with a moustache and cap) working on the roads in Durham City near the Cock of the North pub and restaurant around the 1930s

The wartime wedding of James's daughter Laura Malia and Jacky Ditchburn in 1945

James's fourth son Thomas Malia married Martha Waller in June 1947

James's two youngest daughters had a double wedding on 19 January 1952. Kitty Malia wed Ronnie Barker, and Margaret Malia married Johnny Friend

*James in his garden at Maple
Avenue, Sherburn Road,
Durham City, around 1950s*

*One of the few photos of Mary
Emma and James Malia, at Kitty
and Margaret's joint wedding*

James Malia moved to 23 Maple Avenue, Sherburn Road Estate in about 1936. A new house with a new garden, and proud to be there

THOMAS MALIA (Senior)
Born 27 September 1880

ames Malia (Senior) had a brother called Thomas
(Senior) who was born on 27 September 1880, also at 13
Framwellgate, Durham City. Thomas will have been
christened in St Godric's RC Church, in Framwellgate,
Durham.

EARLY CHILDHOOD
Thomas (Senior) was the second eldest child in the
family. Before Thomas, however, there had been a brother
called Michael who was born 16 July 1879, but he sadly died
only four months later on 17 November of that year. When
Thomas was about six years old, twin brothers were born on 8
May 1886, but they both sadly died too, two months later on
12 July. Infant mortality was very high in the nineteenth
century.

Thomas's surviving siblings were James Malia (Senior)
who was born, as already mentioned, on 2 October 1877;
Catherine, who was born on 19 February 1884; John Malia
(Senior) who was born 13 July 1888; Margaret, born 9 January

1891; and finally Joseph Patrick (Senior) born 28 January 1895.

In the 1881 census, Thomas and the family were recorded as living at Milburngate, Durham with no house number. This was opposite Framwellgate, where he had been born. Moving on to the 1891 census, Thomas was aged around eleven years old then and was recorded as a scholar still living at 13 Framwellgate with his family.

WORKING LIFE

In the 1901 census Thomas was around twenty-one years of age, living at 62 South Street, Durham City with his parents and siblings. He was recorded as a worker, and his occupation was a bricklayer's labourer.

Thomas must have liked gambling because it was recorded in *The County Durham Advertiser* on Friday 10 July that Thomas and a few friends had been caught playing 'banker' and Thomas had been fined 2s/6d.

In the 1911 census, Thomas was living at 111 Framwellgate. He was around thirty years old then and lived in what looks like a multi-dwelling property with other single men. An interesting heading on this census form is one of Profession or Occupation of persons aged ten and upwards. His name is misspelt as Thomas Melia in that census return.

FIRST WORLD WAR

In February 1914 the newspapers ran army recruitment adverts in preparation for World War One. They included a soldier's wages as a private in the regular army, on enlistment:

Cavalry 9s/11d a week. After two years 11s/8d to 13s/5d
Artillery 10s/21/2d a week. After two years 11s/11d to
13s/5d
Infantry 8s/9d a week. After two years 10s/6d to 12s/3d.

On 6 August 1914 the headlines of *The Newcastle Daily Chronicle* were 'Great Britain at War'. On 22 August in *The Evening Chronicle* there was an advert saying, 'Those Who Want to Serve Their Country' and asking for men who were 5 foot 3 inches and up, for the duration of the war. The poster specified ex-soldiers of under forty-two years (because they were experienced) and other men of under thirty. At the bottom was written 'God Save the King'. Posters were put up all over the country aiming to recruit men of all ages. A few will be included at the end of this chapter.

Thomas joined the army and was in the Royal Engineers and Waterways Division (regiment number 340881). On his army forms, it says that Thomas was living at 7 Milburngate, Durham City, and that his previous job was farm labourer working for a farmer called W Gibson from Sherburn, Durham. His height was 5ft 2½ inches and his chest was 33½ inches. His weight was 126 lbs, which was smaller than it said on the recruitment posters. On this form in some places the name is spelt correctly as Malia but elsewhere it is Melia.

Thomas was transferred to the Agricultural Battalion at the end of the war until he was demobbed around March 1919. During his time in the army, Thomas was disciplined in 1918 for being missing from active duty between the times of 0800 hrs and 0815 hrs. He was fined a week's wage, which was roughly 12s 6d. In those days a packet of cigarettes was 3d and a pint of beer was 6d.

After the war Thomas continued working on the farms and lived in the same area he was born.

THOMAS'S DEATH

Sadly, it was reported in *The Sunderland Daily Echo* and *The Shipping Gazette* on 28 March 1933, and in *The Durham Advertiser* on 31 March, that Thomas had been involved in an accident at Low Burnhall Farm, Broompark, Durham. He had died of his injuries on 25 March 1933.

The Sunderland Echo reported a Durham fatality and 'a verdict of accidental death on Thomas Malia (52) of Milburngate, a thresher feeder who died in County Hospital. Malia had suffered a fractured shoulder blade and other injuries in a thresher accident at Low Burnhall Farm, Durham.'

The Durham County Advertiser had a longer report: 'Crushed by Thresher. Inquiry into Fatality at Broompark. Coroner W Carr said that the man was crushed between the steam thresher and gate post. John Thomas Cornforth, thresher proprietor, said, "It was Malia's duty to see the thresher went safely through the gate. I do not know how the accident happened… another man opened the gate, and I did not notice Malia at all." Mr Malia was removed to Durham County Hospital almost immediately.'

James Curry of Cottage Row was walking with the other men a hundred yards away when he heard a shout and ran back and found Malia lying on the road about a yard and a half from the gate post. Medical evidence shows Malia was admitted to hospital from shock and extensive injuries. He never recovered and died in hospital.

The jury returned a verdict of accidental death and expressed the view that Malia had been crushed.

Thomas's death certificate shows he died of 'shock due to fractured right scapula and other injuries'.

Thomas Malia (Senior) is buried at Redhills Roman Catholic Cemetery in Durham City.

THE
MILITARY SERVICE ACT,
1916,

APPLIES TO UNMARRIED MEN WHO, ON AUGUST 15th, 1915, WERE 18 YEARS OF AGE OR OVER AND WHO WILL NOT BE 41 YEARS OF AGE ON MARCH 2nd, 1916.

ALL MEN (NOT EXCEPTED OR EXEMPTED),

between the above ages who, on November 2nd, 1915, were Unmarried or Widowers without any Child dependent on them will, on

Thursday, March 2nd, 1916

BE DEEMED TO BE ENLISTED FOR THE PERIOD OF THE WAR.

They will be placed in the Reserve until Called Up in their Class.

MEN EXCEPTED:

SOLDIERS, including Territorials who have volunteered for Foreign Service;
MEN serving in the NAVY or ROYAL MARINES;
MEN DISCHARGED from ARMY or NAVY, disabled or ill, or TIME-EXPIRED MEN;
MEN REJECTED for the ARMY since AUGUST 14th, 1915;
CLERGYMEN, PRIESTS, and MINISTERS OF RELIGION;
VISITORS from the DOMINIONS.

MEN WHO MAY BE EXEMPTED BY LOCAL TRIBUNALS:

Men more useful to the Nation in their present employments;
Men in whose case Military Service would cause serious hardship owing to exceptional financial or business obligations or domestic position;
Men who are ill or infirm;
Men who conscientiously object to combatant service. If the Tribunal thinks fit, men may, on this ground, be (*a*) exempted from combatant service only (not non-combatant service), or (*b*) exempted on condition that they are engaged in work of National importance.

Up to March 2nd, a man can apply to his Local Tribunal for a certificate of exemption. There is a Right of Appeal. He will not be called up until his case has been dealt with finally.

Certificates of exemption may be absolute, conditional or temporary. Such certificates can be renewed, varied or withdrawn.

Men retain their Civil Rights until called up and are amenable to Civil Courts only.

DO NOT WAIT UNTIL MARCH 2nd.
ENLIST VOLUNTARILY NOW.

In 1916 conscription was introduced because the supply of volunteers like Thomas wasn't enough. Imperial War Museum

JOHN MALIA (Senior)
Born 12 August 1888

John Malia (Senior) was a younger brother of James Malia (Senior) and so his parents were the same, James Malia and Mary Ann (Prendergast) Malia. John was born on 12 August 1888 and was christened at St Godric's RC Church, Framwellgate, Durham City. Records of his christening show his name was recorded in Latin as Lohannes Melia. His parents were down as Jacobi Melia and Mariae Prendergast.

EARLY YEARS

John (Senior) was seventh born in the family. He had three siblings who died before he was born: Michael (born 16 July 1879 and died November 1879) and Michael and Martin (born 6 May 1886, both died 8 July 1886)

His surviving siblings were James Malia (Senior) born on 2 October 1877; Thomas Malia (Senior) who was born on 27 September 1880; Catherine who was born February 1884; Margaret, born in January 1891; and Joseph Patrick (Senior) born January 1895).

In the 1891 census, John was aged two and lived at 13 Framwellgate with his family. Moving onto the 1901 census, records show John aged twelve, living at 62 South Street, Durham City, with his family. When John was nine years old, his mother Mary Malia died on 21 February 1904.

ADULTHOOD

John (Senior) must have liked a drink or two. There are stories about him in *The Durham Advertiser* (although his surname is spelt wrongly as John Melia). On 6 July 1906 he was fined for drunkenness in Milburngate and on 10 July 1908 he was fined five shillings for being drunk and disorderly. It was his sixteenth appearance! It sounds like John Malia knew how to work hard and play hard!

In the 1911 census John lived on his own in a multi-dwelling house, 111 Framwellgate, Durham City. His occupation was a miner.

According to records from the time, miners were paid an average of nine shillings a day, less deductions for equipment, oil lamps, illness and injuries.

FIRST WORLD WAR

In February 1914, adverts started to appear in the newspapers for army recruitment, including their wages and incentives, promotions, holidays and sports.

The Newcastle Daily Chronicle, on Thursday 4 August 1914, reported 'Great Britain at War'. In a special edition of *The Evening Chronicle* on Saturday 22 August 1914, there was an advert for recruits 5ft 3ins high and upwards, chest measurements at least 34 inches, ex regular 19-42 years and other men 19-30 years. For the duration of the war, several types of recruiting posters were placed all over the country to get people to join up to fight.

At the outbreak of the war in 1914, John answered a recruitment poster. As a miner, he preferred the army as it would be a break from the conditions working down the mine.

John was recruited into the Durham Light Infantry 15th Battalion. I was unable to find any of John's army records as they must have been destroyed. His surname was spelt Melia instead of Malia.

On 11 February 1916 John's father, old James Malia, died. Five months later, on 1 July 1916, John was reported missing, presumed dead.

AFTER JOHN'S DEATH

A letter was sent to Mrs Mary Emma Malia (the wife of James Malia (Senior) at 49 Framwellgate, County Durham. It concluded that John Malia was presumed dead and to have died on 1 July. The letter continued, 'Any articles of private property left by the missing soldier are found and forwarded to this office. They cannot be disposed of until authority is received from the war office.' John was only twenty-seven years old when he died.

The records of Soldiers' Effects 1901-1929 show that John's surviving siblings each received a lump sum of money from the army war gratuity on John's behalf, but not until nearly the end of the war. On 6 June 1918, Mrs E Malia of 83 Framwellgate, Durham City received a letter from the War Office, including a payment of 4s /7d, in the settlement of

John's account. The letter and payment were sent to her at the request of her husband James because he was still away fighting in the war.

Letters from the records office were sent to the family on behalf of the King, including medals and decorations. A letter was sent from the Secretary of State for War on behalf of King George V, expressing sympathy.

MEMORIALS

Records with the Commonwealth War Graves Commission show John's surname was spelt Melia. This was corrected in their records in 2004 at the request of the family, who included proof that John's surname was Malia and not Melia.

The CWGC sent photographic evidence of the changes they had made to the Thiepval Memorial in France. John's name is on Pier and Face 14A and 15C. (The memorial location is the Thiepval Memorial, D73, off the main Bapaume to Albert Road D929.)

On the war memorial at St Godric's RC Church, Durham City, the church where John Malia was christened, John's surname is also spelled Melia. A request has been made to get the surname changed to Malia. At the time of writing, the family is waiting for this to be done (June 2020).

The bronze memorial plaque which was issued to John's next of kin. His surname is spelt incorrectly here. These four-inch medals became known as 'dead man's pennies'

John Malia's name on the war memorial at Thiepval, now an MA- in the middle of all the ME-s

The payment of soldier's effects was made to my grandma, Mary Emma Malia, the wife of James Malia (Senior) in 1918

In Memory of
Private
John Malia

15365, 15th Bn., Durham Light Infantry who died on 01 July 1916 Age 27

Son of James and Mary Malia, of 13, Framwellgate, Durham.

Remembered with Honour
Thiepval Memorial

Commemorated in perpetuity by
the Commonwealth War Graves Commission

*Proof of the name change by the Commonwealth War Graves
Commission in 2004*

JOSEPH PATRICK MALIA (Senior)
Born 28 January 1895

Joseph Patrick Malia (Senior) was born 28 January 1895, at 13 Framwellgate, Durham City, County Durham. He was probably baptised at St Godric's RC Church, Durham City (like the rest of his siblings) and went to St Godric's RC School, Durham City. Joseph was the youngest in his family. When he was only nine, Joseph's mother died, on 21 February 1904. Around 1909 Joseph was becoming a bit of a handful for his father. It was recorded in a letter around 1921 that 'he hadn't been doing the right thing' by his oldest brother James Malia (Senior).

MOVING HOME
It was decided that Joseph Patrick would go to live with his aunt, Margaret (Prendergast) Clark, and her family at 24 Victoria Street, Shotton Colliery, Castle Eden, County Durham. At this address in the 1911 census Joseph was recorded as a coal miner driver.

FIRST WORLD WAR

On 5 August 1914, Joseph Patrick (Senior), along with his cousins whose surname was Clark, enlisted to fight in World War One, just like a lot of miners did. His name too was recorded as Joseph Clark on his enlistment papers. His height was 5 foot 4½ inches, and his weight was 124 lbs, chest 35 inches. He was enlisted to the Durham Light Infantry, 2nd Battalion (service number 11769). When he finished his training, he was sent to France on the front line.

This is where Joseph Patrick met up with his eldest brother James Malia (Senior) who was also in the DLI 2nd Battalion. According to the letter dated 1918 and written by James, both of them had talked about getting Joseph's surname corrected to Malia. At this point they went to their sergeant major to try and get it changed. Sadly, before this was done their brother John Malia was killed in action on 1 July 1916. He had been serving with the DLI 15th Battalion.

On 11 February 1916 their father old James Malia had died back home in Durham City. Joseph Patrick himself was killed in action on 23 June 1917 in Flanders. His name, however, was recorded as Joseph Clark in the British service records 1914-1920.

AFTER HIS DEATH

On 23 November 1919, Joseph Patrick's brother, James Malia (Senior), wrote a letter to the Army Records Office. He requested that his brother's name be changed from Joseph Clark to Joseph Patrick Malia, and his medals and anything else be forwarded to him to share with the rest of his siblings.

The medals were sent to the family and the army payroll had him recorded as Joseph Clark alias Joseph Patrick Malia. His pay was shared with his siblings with each receiving as follows: Thomas Malia (£9/1s/10d), Margaret (Malia) Moore (£8/17s/ 2d), Catherine (Malia) Wellford (£9/1s/9d), Mary E (Fowler) Malia (request of her husband James Malia £9/1s/9d).

Joseph Patrick's headstone was erected at Maroc British Cemetery, Grenay, Pas de Calais, France 11. D. 12. It had the inscription DLI 11769 Private J. Clark Durham Light Infantry 23rd June 1917.

On 2 February 2017, Joseph Patrick's great-nephew, John Malia (Author), made a request to the Commonwealth War Graves Commission asking for their records to be changed and the headstone to be changed from Joseph Clark to Joseph Patrick Malia. Included with the letter were all the records and information he had on Joseph Patrick Malia. On 10 February, John received a letter from CWGC informing him they had amended their records to Joseph Patrick Malia with an alias of Joseph Clark. They would also change the headstone and inform John when this was done.

On the 28 April 2017, CWGC informed John that they had now changed the headstone, with a photo of the change. The headstone now reads, 'J P Malia, served as J Clark, Durham Light Infantry, 23 June 1917, age 22.'

An example of a First World War recruiting poster from the Imperial War Museum

The original and the corrected gravestones of Private J P
Malia, also known as J Clark

SECOND
GENERATION
OF THE
MALIA FAMILY

JOHN MALIA (Junior)
Born 29 December 1919

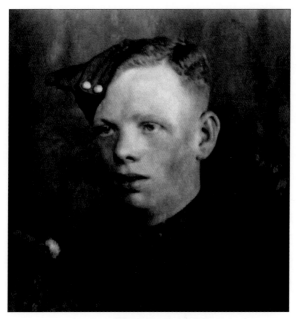

John Malia (Junior)

M y father was one of the second generation of his family to be born in England. His name was John Malia and he was born on 29 December 1919 at 83 Framwellgate, Durham City. His father was James Malia (Senior) and his mother was Mary Emma.

John Malia (Junior) was christened at St Godric's RC Church, Durham. He had four brothers and four sisters: James (born 1909), Allan John (born 1911), Mary (born 1914), Joseph Patrick (Junior) (born 1917), Thomas (Junior) (born 1921), Laura (born 1924), Kitty (born 1928) and Margaret (born 1931).

EARLY YEARS

John Malia (Junior) started school at the age of five at St Godric's RC School in Framwellgate, Durham City. He left school at the age of fourteen (equivalent to leaving at the end of Year 9 today). In the early 1930s, the family moved from the Framwellgate, Milburngate area of Durham to Sherburn Road Estate, about a mile from the city centre.

The family were named in the 1939 Register, living at Maple Avenue, Sherburn Road Estate, Durham City. The 1939 Register was taken in the United Kingdom, on the 29 September 1939 at the outbreak of war, for the introduction of identity cards and ration books. This register was in addition to the ten-year census and was a way of recording everyone living in Great Britain at the time. This led to the internment of mostly Germans and Italians, who were considered to be potential enemies of the state.

After leaving school, my father John started working at

Cocken Drift Mine, near the banks of the River Wear, although he only worked there for a short while. This type of mine was not very deep and the miners could walk straight to the coal seams. This was his first job in the mines. He then went on to work at Brandon Pit House Colliery in a small village about two miles from Durham city centre, where he still lived. John worked there as a coal cutter. This was one of the most dangerous jobs in the mine, working right at the coal seam deep underground. After the coal was cut out, a hewer would load the coal into tubs, to be taken to the surface, sometimes by pit ponies. John worked there from 1933 until he was called up with his brother Joseph Patrick (Junior) at the start of World War Two in 1941.

SECOND WORLD WAR

John was recruited into the army as a private in the Royal Engineers. His unit was called the African Pioneer Corps. He was based in Palestine, along with many other units in the British army.

John's brother, Joseph Patrick, was recruited as a gunner in the Royal Artillery. On 5 June 1942, Joseph was out on patrol with his unit when they were ambushed. Joseph was shot and captured by Italian troops and died the next day from his wounds. Before he went to war, he had told his mam, 'Don't you worry, ma, the Germans will never catch me alive.'

During the war, John was attached to several units. One of his jobs was to detonate unwanted explosives that were left over by the enemy at captured territory in Knightsbridge, Acroma, Libya. One day, he was detonating with explosives on the edge of a cemetery in the Middle East. Because of slow communications during the war, John didn't know that his brother Joseph Patrick had been wounded and had already died. He later found out that his brother was actually buried in that cemetery. He regretted not knowing this, and used to say, 'If I had known, I would have gone to visit his grave.'

At the end of the war, John stayed in the army, working in the post room as a sorter and also as a physical training instructor. One of his final jobs was an unexploded bomb instructor. John was demobbed from the army in 1946.

AFTER THE WAR

On coming home, John picked up where he had left off and started working in the mines again. From 30 September 1946 to 11 February 1950, John worked as a cutter again, at Kimblesworth Colliery.

In 1946 there were approximately eight hundred private colliery companies, but after the war the UK Government decided that these companies should be nationalised. On 12 July 1946 the Nationalisation of Coal Mines Act was introduced, and on 1 January 1947 all the mining companies were transferred to the National Coal Board (NCB).

John transferred from Kimblesworth to Brandon Pit House Colliery as a face worker on 11 February 1950 and continued working there until 2 November 1957.

After having health problems with his back, from several accidents down the mines, John transferred jobs and became a gate end operator for a short period of time in 1957. He was then transferred to the supplies stores from November 1957 to

February 1962. From February 1962 he worked as a general worker until he was pensioned out of the mines on the 22 October 1965.

During his time at the pits, John worked on local farms as a labourer on his days off. One of the farms he worked on was for a farmer called Dickie Hopps. On these farms, John milked the cows, planted crops and at harvest time would join in the harvesting, before sorting the goods ready to go to market.

Johns' health improved and he felt he could manage lighter work than mining. He looked for work in the local factories where he lived and started work as a wool winder in a carpet factory called Hugh Mackay's, at Dragonville, Gilesgate, Durham City. He worked there from 1968 to 1971. This is where I had my first job. My dad then got a job at a local plastics factory Mono Containers, Dragonville, Gilesgate, as a packer, working permanent night shifts. He worked on this job from 1971 until he started having health problems again, mainly with his back, so he went on sick leave until his retirement in 1974.

MARRIED LIFE

After he had been demobbed from the army and returned home, John met his wife Bridget Casey, who lived on the same housing estate. Bridget was friends with John's sister Laura.

My mother was always known as Biddy. She was born on 2 May 1926. When my parents' families moved house from the city centre, they both went to live on the same housing estate. My mother went to St Cuthbert's RC Junior and Infants School, and St Leonard's RC Secondary School.

After my mother left school, she had several jobs, including working as a window cleaner with her father. During the war, she worked in an ammunition factory.

John and Bridget started courting and got married on 5 April 1947 at St Cuthbert's RC Church. At the beginning of their married life, they lived with John's parents in Maple Avenue on Sherburn Road Estate, until they found their own place at Jacob's Ladder, in Durham City. Here was where their first two children were born, Joseph Patrick (January 1948) and Bridget Mary (July 1949).

In 1950 they moved to a three-bedroom house on Goodyear Crescent, on Sherburn Road Estate. In June 1950 their third child was born, Veronica Theresa. They really enjoyed this home; it had gardens back and front, and a bathroom inside with a bath, toilet and sink. John used the front garden to plant flowers and in the back he would plant vegetables. He also kept hens for their eggs and occasionally one for the pot.

In March 1953 John and Bridget's fourth child was born, Bernadette. With his eldest three children, John had a very strict bedtime rule; up until the age of eleven, the three of them had to be in bed no later than six o'clock at night.

In April of that year, John and a work mate were involved in a fall of stone down the pit at Pit House Colliery, Brandon. John injured his back and was sent to hospital. Sadly, his friend Alfred (Alfie) Newton, aged forty-seven, was killed. Both had started working down the pit at fourteen years old at Kimblesworth Colliery. The story of the accident was reported in *The Durham Advertiser* on 24 April 1953.

My father told all of his children about this accident over

the years. He was working on a seam with his colleague Alfie when they heard a large rumble and a crashing sound. John moved as quick as he could into the seam, and Alfie tried to get out. Alfie was caught by the fall of stone and was killed, and John was trapped in the seam. He lay there for about an hour until the mine rescue team broke a small hole into the fall of stone. Then John heard a voice.

'John, John, are you in there?' the man shouted.

'I'm in here. Get me out!' John replied. The man shouting was part of the mine rescue team. He was called Cud Heseltine, and also lived on Sherburn Road Estate. John said it must have taken at least three hours for the hole to be made big enough to get him out. He told us that Cud sat on the other side of the fall of stone, all the time talking and keeping him calm until he could finally be rescued. He never forgot the accident, or Cud for staying with him in such a dire situation.

John was in hospital for about a week after the accident. When he got home, there was a constant stream of people from the NCB and the union, coming to the door wanting statements from John about the accident. This continued right up until the inquest for poor Alfie Newton, who left behind a grieving family.

I AM BORN!

In April 1956 a fifth child was born to John Malia (Junior) and his wife Bridget, and that was myself, John Malia. I was named after my dad, who was also the fifth child born to his parents. We were now a family of seven living in the same house. In June 1958 their sixth and final child was born,

Denise, the baby of the family.

When my brother, Joseph Patrick, and I were around eight years old, we used to ask questions like, 'Did you ever shoot anybody in the war? What's it like to shoot someone?' The reply was always the same: 'I don't know. When you're getting fired at you lift your gun and fire back not looking to see if you have hit anyone. And don't ask questions like that.'

Then Dad would tell us that his unit used to get called to check for mines to be cleared to make it safe for the troops. He would then go into how it was done. Firstly, he would get a knife from the kitchen drawer, and tell us this would be his bayonet removed from his rifle. He would give us the knife to copy his actions, and we then laid on the floor. 'Put your knife at an angle and gently push it into the ground,' he told us. Then he would shout, 'Stop, we've found something!'

The next thing to do with the 'bayonet' was gently feel around with it. Dad told us that once you had established that it was a mine, you gently moved the soil around the edges. Once this was done, you had to check underneath to make sure it wasn't booby-trapped with a wire or anchored so that if you lifted it, it would detonate the mine.

Once all this was done, you put a flag by it with different colours; one for if it could be lifted and made safe, and a different one for if it was booby-trapped and had to be detonated on the spot. Then a sweep team would follow behind and deal with them in the appropriate way for each mine.

Afterwards Dad and his mates would look back and wonder how they had kept so calm. Every time they were given a job like that, they would have to report to the mess.

While they were being told about the operation, they were given a large mug of tea. They always thought after the war that something must have been put in the tea to keep them calm.

In 1982 Britain was at war with Argentina, after they had invaded the Falkland Islands. The British Government sent a task force to claim them back. The war lasted seventy-seven days until the Argentine forces surrendered to the British. By the end, 237 British service people had lost their lives.

After the Falklands War, the British Government said that anyone who was a direct family member of a service person who had died and was buried there could go with one other and visit their grave. My dad John Malia (Junior), who had served in the Second World War, wrote to the Ministry of Defence in 1983 asking if he could go as a representative of the family to visit his brother's grave in Libya. He explained his story of how he had blown explosives up next to the cemetery during World War Two, not knowing that his brother was buried there, and how he would have liked to have visited back then.

Dad received a letter back from the MOD explaining that peacetime arrangements for people visiting graves of relatives killed in conflicts had not been made until 1967, and the graves had to be visited within two years of the death. It went on to say that they would like to let relatives of service people killed during World War Two visit their graves, but the numbers would be so large that the government could not afford it. John was a bit disappointed, but accepted the reply.

There was danger for my dad on the home front too. Around 1964 my dad was in his kitchen helping with our meal.

He picked up the frying pan from the cooker and went to take it to the sink. Suddenly the pan fell off from the handle and onto his foot, spilling hot fat. He let out a scream of, 'Cow in hell!' as he wouldn't swear in front of us. We kids thought it was funny, our dad jumping about like a cartoon character and shouting. But we didn't laugh because we knew if we had, we would have got it wrong, because it was quite serious.

Our mam immediately poured vinegar on the burn, and made it worse. Eventually Dad poured cold water on it and put a bandage on. It took a couple of weeks before it started to heal. After that, they never bought cheap pans and kept checking the handles on a regular basis.

There was another time we thought was funny but didn't dare laugh. Dad went up into the attic to get the Christmas decorations. While he was up there, we heard a crack and a bang. We rushed upstairs only to see a pair of legs dangling through a large hole in the ceiling. Our mam gave him a hand to get out but luckily he had only skinned his shins. The next day they had to get the council to come and repair the damage.

In the mid-sixties, Dad and I decided to get some racing pigeons and race them in the local club. We raced for about four years, and during that time were quite successful. The pigeons regularly finished in the first four positions.

On each race, you found out what time the birds had been liberated. After this you were told what the weather conditions were, and what speed and direction the wind was. Then you could work out roughly what time the birds were expected. You would be ready at your loft at least thirty minutes before they were due back.

The birds were always sent off wearing a rubber ring on

their legs with a number stamped on it for identification. When they returned, you would take the rings off and place them into a container which was then put into a compartment in the clock. You'd press a lever on the clock to record their times.

One day we were getting things ready at the loft and I saw a pigeon coming in.

'There's one coming!' I shouted as it dropped. I got the bird into the loft and took the ring off.

'The clock's not here!' Dad shouted to my mam. 'Biddy, get the clock. It's in the house.' Mam brought the clock box out but when Dad opened it, it was the empty box with no clock inside. He rushed into the house with the ring, found the clock and stamped it into the clock. Our bird came in third. If we'd had the clock on hand that day, we might have won the race. After that, the loft was always ready well before the pigeons were due back. Years later we would have a good laugh about it, but at the time we didn't think it was very funny.

In the late sixties and early seventies, Dad started going to the local bingo hall (which used to be the old cinema) before he went for a drink at the New Durham Club. On the odd night, he would win a few pounds and when he was on his way back home, he would call in at the local fish and chip shop and treat us all to fish and chips.

When Dad had been out for a couple of drinks in New Durham Working Men's Club, he would often come in and recite the poem 'Gunga Din' by Rudyard Kipling. Gunga Din was a servant to an officer in the British Army in India in the 1890s. The officer treated him very badly but one day the officer was shot and Gunga gave him water and saved his life.

The officer was so grateful for this that he wrote about Gunga Din. He regretted his past actions against his servant and in the end, he thought Gunga was the better man than he. This inspired Rudyard Kipling to write the poem. I don't know where my dad learnt this poem, but he could recite the whole of it without hesitation.

In 1969 my eldest sister Bridget married Rod Rodwell at St Joseph's RC Church on Mill Lane, Gilesgate. This was soon followed by my eldest brother, Joseph Patrick, marrying Sandra Jones at the chapel in New Brancepeth in the summer of 1970. In the autumn of the same year, Theresa was married to Allan Mathers, also at St Joseph's RC Church. A few years later in 1974, Bernadette married Allan Clark at St Joseph's. In 1977 mum and dad's youngest son John (that's me) was married to Amanda (Mandy) Smith at Mary Magdalen Church, Belmont, Durham City. Finally, Denise, my youngest sister, married Barry Comby at Durham Register Office.

John and Bridget soon had thirteen grandchildren: Joe and Sandra's daughters, Joanna and Tracy; Bridget and Rod's daughters, Shoshana and Natalia Rodwell; Theresa and Allan's son and daughter, Richard and Carolyn Mathers; Bernadette and Allan's son and daughter, James and Victoria Clark; our sons, Benjamin and Matthew; and finally Denise and Barry's sons, William, Wayne and Nathan Comby.

Later, two more grandchildren came along as Bernadette and Alan Clark had another son, Andrew, in 1990.

Sadly in 1993 Joseph's wife Sandra died. A few years later Joseph met Margaret Walker, and later had a son with her in 1995, another John. Joe and Margaret were married in 1998.

Around 1983, my dad decided to have a go at flying

racing pigeons again from a loft in his back garden. He bought a new loft and started to train the pigeons, then joined the local racing pigeon club. He raced for about three years and was quite successful.

In 1984 John celebrated his sixty-fifth birthday with a party for all his family and neighbours, including some of his eldest grandchildren. This was the last big family gathering he had. He also had to stop racing pigeons around 1986, because his health had deteriorated.

THE DEATH OF JOHN MALIA (Junior)

Over the next two years, my dad John was in and out of hospital. When he was admitted in late November 1987, the doctors diagnosed him with terminal cancer. Sadly, on 31 December 1987, John died at Dryburn Hospital, Durham City. On that day we were all at the hospital visiting, his six children and our mam. Mam had been at the hospital most of the day and we kept saying to her that she should go home for a bit and get some rest. She said, 'I'll go home, if you all do. I'll get some rest, if you leave with me. Let your dad get some rest.' We decided to do what Mam wanted, and left.

After about an hour, Mam got the phone call from the hospital that Dad had died. It was New Year's Eve. I had popped back home to see Mandy and the boys and that's where I was when I got a call from my brother Joseph to tell me about Dad.

Normally on a New Year's Eve, Mandy and I would have a party. The boys and family and friends would come. We had been doing this for a number of years. As I was telling the boys about their grandad, I started feeling a bit emotional. Our youngest son Matthew, aged five at the time, paused for a while and then asked, 'Does that mean Grandad won't be coming to our party tonight?' We had to explain to him to help him understand. In the end, we went ahead and had our New Year's Eve party to cheer ourselves up.

John's funeral service was held at St Joseph's RC Church, Mill Lane, Gilesgate, Durham City. He was buried in a double grave at South Road Crematorium, Durham City.

After Dad passed away, our mam Bridget stayed on living in their home until 2015, when she had an accident and broke her leg. She went to Dryburn Hospital for about two weeks and was later transferred to Bishop Auckland Hospital, County Durham. She was then transferred to St Aidan's Care Home, Framwellgate Moor, in Durham, where she was diagnosed with severe vascular dementia.

Mum was finally transferred to Willington Care Home, County Durham for the rest of her days. Sadly, our mam, Bridget Malia, died there on 24 September 2018. Like Dad, she also had her funeral service at St Joseph's RC Church. My parents are now both in the same grave, back together again! God rest their souls.

*Joseph Patrick Malia (Junior), my uncle,
ready to go off to war in 1941*

John Malia (Junior) and Bridget Casey at their wedding, 5 April 1947

*My father John Malia, second from right, on a break
during mine clearances, 1944*

My father, John Malia, in uniform

*A family gathering at John Malia's sixty-fifth
birthday*

THIRD GENERATION OF THE MALIA FAMILY

JOHN MALIA (Author)
Born 17 April 1956

The author as a young boy

I was born John Malia, on 17 April 1956. My family lived at 29 Goodyear Crescent, Sherburn Road Estate, Durham City. I was christened at St Joseph's RC Church, Mill Lane, in Gilesgate and was the fifth child born into the family. I have an elder brother, three elder sisters and a younger sister.

After my dad was demobbed in 1945, he started getting back into normal life again. He met and started courting my mother in the summer of 1946. They married the next April and rented a tenement in Claypath in the city centre. In 1950 they moved their forever-home on Goodyear Crescent on Sherburn Road Estate, which was rented from the council. There were three bedrooms in our home: Mam and Dad had one bedroom, my sisters shared a bedroom and my brother and I shared a room. Later, when my brother Joseph started drinking alcohol after a night out, he would come in drunk and wake me up, prodding me and talking about things. I didn't have a clue what he was on about. I was glad when he got married because I had the room to myself.

My siblings are Joseph Patrick Malia, Bridget Mary Malia, Veronica Theresa Malia, Bernadette Malia and Denise Malia. The three eldest siblings were born within two years and eleven months of each other.

CHILDHOOD

One of my first memories is of starting to walk, and my mam shouting to our next-door neighbour, Mrs Pledger, 'Come and see! He's starting to walk!' Mam told me they were worried about me because I was nearly two and still didn't walk; that's why she was so excited.

One of the games we used to play at home was seeing how many of our stairs we could jump down. I was about eight years old at the time. Our Theresa, who was about thirteen years old, went to the top one day and jumped all the way to the bottom (about fourteen steps in total). When she landed, she hurt her ankle and had to go to the hospital. She came back with a cast on as she had broken it. Of course, you can guess that we were never allowed to play that game again.

Around 1961, we were all very excited because we were getting our first television. Before that we used to go down to my granny Malia's house on a Saturday afternoon to watch the wrestling. Her TV had a ten-inch screen built into a cabinet about two feet by three feet, and the picture was black and white. When ours arrived, it was about a nineteen-inch screen on legs with no large cabinet, still black and white pictures, and two channels, Channel One on BBC, and Channel 8 from Tyne Tees Television. There wasn't much choice what to watch and at 10 pm the channels both closed down and played 'God Save the Queen' to mark the end of the day. We thought we were very posh at the time. What a difference from today when TVs have screens of up to sixty inches, with colour, and multiple channels going on twenty-four hours a day.

During the six weeks school summer holidays, our mam and dad used to take us on a service bus to Crimdon Dene for the day. This was on the coast about forty minutes' drive away. We were very happy, and we used to play in the Dene and go down to the beach and splash around in the water. There was a pavilion building where you could buy food and drinks and get out of the rain. It also had a small show field with a few slot machines that used the old penny. We would spend the day there and go home around five o'clock. At the bus stops there were hundreds of people queuing to get back home.

We went on an overnight holiday in the mid-60s to Blackpool for the Illuminations. It was a great day out. I can still remember the boarding house we stayed in; it was number 23 Blundell Street. This was a great treat that my dad had earned by selling tickets for the trip.

My dad worked as a miner and every month he would get an allowance of coal from the National Coal Board. The wagon dropped it off at the front of the house, and all of us helped take it round the back using a barrow and buckets. We would fill up the coal house, which was under the stairs. If there was any coal left over, the neighbours would come and pay us thre'pence a bucket. It didn't take long to sell all of the coal, and we would get some pocket money from it.

When I was seven, we would go and get our granny Malia's shopping from the local store every Saturday. When we took it back, our gran would give us spending money of a thre'pence.

My dad used to keep hens in the back garden for a few years for the eggs and meat. I remember one day, he killed one of them to be cooked for a meal. To do this, he chopped its head off then laid it on the ground. The poor headless hen got up and staggered round for a little bit, then sat down and laid an egg. Lastly, she rolled over onto her side, which I thought looked very funny at the time. We ate the fowl that night!

Behind the local shops, there was a scout hut. When I was around seven years old, I went to join the local cubs. The lady in charge stood in the doorway and said, 'You can't join.

You're a Catholic. You lot can't swear allegiance to the Queen.' I don't think that would happen today.

From seven to about ten years old, we used to go to the local picture house, the Majestic, on a Saturday morning, to watch the latest children's films. I think it cost about sixpence, so we could only go if we had pocket money. I remember once it was showing a 3D film and we were given special cardboard glasses, with one side red and the other green. It was like we could touch the people in the film, and it felt amazing! Nearly all the children from the estate went to that picture house back then. At the beginning of the 1970s it was closed and became a bingo ball, and this year, 2021, plans have been made to demolish it and build student flats there.

On the estate, there was a large hut which housed the local youth club. We went after school every night from ten to fifteen years old and it probably kept us out of trouble.

In 1966 when England hosted the football World Cup, the Russian and Italian teams were based in the North East, playing their games at Roker Park, Sunderland and Ayresome Park, Middlesbrough. Durham University offered their training grounds at Maiden Castle for them to train. They backed onto Sherburn Road Estate, where I lived, so we used to go down and watch them practise. The Russian goalkeeper, Lev Yashin, gave a pair of his goalkeeping gloves to the boy who lived next door to me. Russia got to the semi-finals, but of course England went on to win it.

When I was about twelve years old, I joined the Air Training Corp, which was in the city centre next to the ice rink. I went two nights a week and was with them for about a year. I learnt quite a bit from them about survival techniques; how to use rifles from World War One; and discipline.

Since I was in the city centre, I also started going to the ice rink, and taught myself how to skate. I only had one accident, when I fell over and knocked myself out. My father would always patch us up when we came home with cuts and bruises. He was from a time when you tried to cure your own ailments by using home remedies. I can remember that he put iodine on cuts (equivalent to TCP today but probably a hundred times stronger). It really stung, but it did the job eventually. Another thing I remember is that if you got a headache, he would get out a little round bottle and you would have to take a big sniff and it would feel like the top of your head was going to blow off...but it did cure your headache. I think it was called snuff. It's probably illegal today.

My friends and I went to the ice rink regularly, until we wanted to start underage drinking, and trying to get into the pubs in the city centre instead.

About 1960 my uncle Jim's dog had pups. They were sheep dog collie crosses, and I was allowed to pick one to keep. I carried it all the way back to our house and named it Dutch. It lived in a kennel outside our back door but would not come into the house. Dutch was knocked over when she was about six or seven. When I was going to take her for a walk, I'd rattle her lead at the back door and Dutch would run over. This particular day, I didn't know that she was in the field over the road when I called her. She darted right across the street and was knocked over. The driver took us to the vets. She had hurt her back legs, but she got over it.

We continued to go on walks until Dutch's health started to deteriorate when she was around twelve years old. By the time she was fourteen years old, her back legs wouldn't always work. After coming home from work one day, I told my dad that it was time Dutch was put to sleep. He said, 'If you want to take her to the vets and do it, you can'.

Being eighteen years old, I thought I could take on the world, so I took her to the vets, lifted her onto the vet's table and said to the vet, 'She's suffering too much, and she needs to be put down'. He put the needle into her leg, I put my money on the table, and then I walked out.

When I got back to the house, my dad said, 'Everything all right?' I just nodded, went up to my bedroom and cried my eyes out. I learnt then that men do cry. I am now sixty-five years old and still remember my dog fondly.

During the 1960s, several of our neighbours had motorbikes. I used to love just sitting on them, but I got lucky one day when a neighbour took me to watch Newcastle United play Manchester United at their home ground. George Best, one of the most talented football players in the world, was on the team. It was one of my favourite days out.

Like most of Britain, 21 October 1966, sticks in my mind. In Aberfan, Wales, 144 people were killed, 116 of whom were children. A coal-mine spoil tip had collapsed under heavy rain, and buried a school. You couldn't believe the news: people digging through the rubble with their bare hands, in tears, looking for survivors. The children were the same age as me.

In the late 1960s, my dad and I started racing pigeons at the local club. We had a pigeon cree (loft) in our back garden. We did quite well, and for three years we won a few races, even getting in the top four! With no car, however, I had to walk six miles along the mid-construction A1M motorway, with several pigeons in a pram base. If I was lucky, I could use my three-pigeon carrying box and catch the local bus to Redcar on the coast. I would release them one at a time, in five-minute intervals. This was to prepare the birds for 'flying over the water' from France.

Once, a pigeon came back with a broken leg so we made a splint out of a cigarette box. When we took it off, she had a limp, and earned the name 'Limpy'. She went on to win a few races, and bred some winners, too. She was more like a pet, following my mam around as she hung up washing. Even after we stopped racing and sold the other birds, we kept Limpy. A friend took her in later, and she bred winners for him, too.

During my teenage summers, my friends and I used to camp in the local meadows. We wandered in the woods and along the riverbanks, trying - and mostly failing - to fish and catch rabbits. We went swimming in a place we called San Diego, because it had a large sandy bank down to the river. The strong swimmers in our large group kept an eye out for the non-swimmers, of which I was one. When we came home, we were all shattered after not getting much sleep.

We called the school holiday in October 'taytey picking' week. Other areas called it half term or blackberry week. In the early morning, the whole town would stand at the top of the estate, waiting for the local farmers to turn up with their tractors and trailers. They would pick who they wanted and, if you were lucky, you jumped into the trailer and went potato picking for the day. You would be paid ten shillings and could fill your haversack with potatoes when you finished working. At the time I also did an evening paper round six nights a week, for seven shillings and sixpence.

SCHOOL DAYS

I started my first school in 1961. It was St Cuthbert's RC Infant and Juniors, in Elvet, Durham City, and I had to catch the bus to get there. I got off at the Porters stop and walked to school over the Old Baths bridge. There were two gates into the yard: one for boys and one for girls. The whole first-year infants (reception class today) had to go in through the girls' gate.

When I attended this school, I still couldn't tie my shoelaces, and ended up tripping on the stone steps and splitting open my chin. My teacher, Mrs Doyle, took me to hospital, and I was patched together with four stitches, and a piece of chocolate for being brave. Every Wednesday afternoon, all pupils had to attend St Cuthbert's RC Church for Mass. I don't remember much about this school as I was so young, and anyway we were only there for less than a year. The building still stands, although it was sold a few years ago and converted into a house.

I next attended St Joseph's RC Infant and Juniors on Mill Lane, Gilesgate, in Durham from 1961 to 1967. This was a brand-new school, and it was only a short walk from my home. Our class put on *Snow White and the Seven Dwarfs* and I played one of the dwarfs, probably because I was so small!

When I was nine years old, three lads in my class broke a desk. The headmaster, Mr Tobin, came in and said I must have done it because I looked guilty. I got four strikes of the cane across my hands, for nothing!

In the mid-sixties, the school organised a day trip for all the pupils. We went to Bamburgh on the Northumberland coast, about fifty miles away. That felt like going to the other side of the world! It cost half a crown, and you were entered into a draw to win ten shillings of spending money. Bamburgh was one of the best places I had been to at that time, and I loved the beach and the few shops there. I returned a few years ago with my wife and grandchildren and saw that time had not changed the town. There were still few shops, a lovely beach, and a castle. It cost more than half a crown, though!

This school was Roman Catholic, so at the age of seven you were prepared to make your First Confession and Holy Communion. We had to confess our sins to a priest in a confessional box and ask for God's forgiveness. Father Olsen would tell us which prayers to say, and how many times. After this, we received Holy Communion at Mass.

A new church was built next to the school as the old one had been in the school hall. It opened the same year we received our First Communion, so we were the first pupils to complete the sacrament there. At the age of seven, we put down our names on a waiting list to become altar boys. I never became an altar boy, but instead the headmaster asked four of us if we would like to weed the priest's garden once a week during our lunchtime break. We did this for the rest of the school year. Some of the teachers I liked, and some I can't remember at all, but overall, it was a fairly good school.

From the age of eleven I went to St Leonard's RC Secondary Modern in North End, Durham. I started there in 1967 and went through to 1971, although in 1970 it became a comprehensive.

When I started this school, I was four foot tall, which was small even for that time. I looked young, but I was no angel at this school! Several times, I got the cane on my hands and bum. One incident that sticks in my mind happened when I was thirteen years old. I was in the toilet at the same time as two other boys, who were smoking in the corner. A teacher came in and caught them, but said, 'You as well, Malia. Up to my classroom!'

I hadn't done anything, but he said he was going to cane me four times across my backside. He hit me once, and then I just ran away as it hurt like hell! He didn't chase me, so I think he realised that he had been too hard. I had PE the next lesson, and the lads noticed blood on my underpants. The teacher had split my bum! If something like this had happened today, the teacher would be arrested. Corporal punishment wasn't banned until 1986.

As I was getting into bed that night, my brother saw the blood as well, and told my mam. I told her that I had done nothing. Whether she believed me or not, she still thought hitting someone that hard was too harsh. The next day, she complained to the headmaster, who had actually taught my mam as well.

'He may have got it for nothing, but there are plenty of things he has got away with,' he said. It was left at that.

When my mam got home, she told me off for all the trouble I had been getting into that she didn't know about. My mam was nobody's fool. When my siblings and I were telling white lies to get out of trouble, she would often say, 'I'm too old of a cat to be caught out by kittens.' She used that one all her life, even with her great-grandchildren.

We often played football in PE. I wanted to be on the school team, but I didn't have the skills. I enjoyed running, though, and got onto the athletic and cross-country team. In my third year (or Year 9), I raced 120 boys from different schools in the Durham district. The track was along the riverbanks, and local school children acted as stewards, pointing us where to go. When I was halfway round, in thirteenth place, I stopped with some stewards from my estate. They were smoking, so I had a 'tab' with them. I finished the race after that and still came twenty-sixth. It was normal for us to smoke. We used to buy one cigarette and a few matches for thre'pence.

In my last year at St Leonard's, we learned about the new decimal currency in maths lessons. In 1971 the UK changed from the old money of pounds, shillings and pennies, to the new decimal currency of pounds and pence. It caused lots of confusion at first, until people got used to it. The government issued cards with money conversions, and posters were put up in shops to help people understand the change.

In the old money, we had a ten shilling note and in the decimal system this was a fifty pence coin. The old coins were half a penny, one penny, threepence, sixpence, one shilling, two shillings, half a crown and a crown (which was five shillings). The new decimal coins were half pence (which was withdrawn from circulation in December 1984), one pence, two pence, five pence, ten pence, fifty pence and the pound note, which was taken out of circulation in 1984 and replaced by a one pound coin.

AFTER SCHOOL DAYS

After I left school at the age of fifteen, I managed to get a job as an apprentice fitter and turner at Hugh MacKay's carpet factory, in Axminster End, Claypath, Durham City. I had to wear overalls, but I couldn't find any that fitted me, so I bought the smallest bib and brace overalls I could find, and tied a knot on the straps. People said I looked like Huckleberry Finn, so I was nicknamed 'Huck' the whole time I worked there.

The other lads in the fitting shop couldn't believe how small I was, so they measured and weighed me. I was five foot tall and weighed five stone. They made a mark on a girder for my height. I grew six inches in the next six months.

We were paid cash in an envelope, with how much you had earned and how much had been taken off for tax and National Insurance. Thursday was payday and after my first week, I got my pay along with the other apprentices. Their take-home pay was £6.53, but mine was £29.59. This was a fortune and I was really excited. Then I found out that I had also received my father's pay, as he worked there, too. I ended up with £6.53, the correct amount. My mam then took a fiver for my board and lodgings, so I was left with only £1.53.

I enjoyed working at MacKay's for two and a half years. When I turned eighteen, however, I would have had to work on a three-shift system, which I did not want to do. The wage would have been only thirteen pounds a week after tax, and my board would have gone up as my pay increased,

It was at this time that we thought because we were working, we were old enough to go out drinking. Because I was quite small, however, I struggled getting into pubs with my friends. So I used to go out and try to get into pubs by myself.

One Friday night, I found one! It had a back room with a

little serving hatch, and I ordered a brown ale. I sat there all night and had three bottles.

The next week I told my friends that I had found a pub I could get into, and that I'd had seven drinks. We all went the next Friday. I went up to the hatch and said to the landlady, 'The usual, please, Molly.' I was trying to impress my friends. I drank nine bottles of brown ale and stayed there until half-past nine.

I can remember heading home, and getting halfway across the passage. My next memory is of my dad waking me up for work, and telling me to come straight home afterwards. I had to go down to the police station. Apparently, I had wandered off from my friends and had been arrested for being 'drunk and incapable'. Since I was underage, the police went to my parents' house at midnight, and my mam had to come pick me up from the station. I had to go back the next day to be charged. I ended up going to court and was fined £1.10.

After that, I learned my lesson with drinking. I never bragged about how much I could drink again, and tried to be more sensible.

I still didn't get into the pubs too often, though. In 1972, I went to Sunderland to go to the Top Rank nightclub. The bouncer stopped me and asked for my age. I said I was eighteen.

He asked what my date of birth was, and quick as a flash, I said, '17 April 1954.'

'Where do you live?' he asked me next.

'Durham,' I said.

Then he quickly asked me, 'How much National Insurance do you pay at work?'

'Sixty-seven pence,' I fired back. Then I realised my mistake. National Insurance for over eighteens was eighty-eight pence a week.

The bouncer laughed. 'For your effort, I'll let you in. But no drinking beer and keep away from the other bouncers. Make sure you get the Durham bus at the end of the night.'

I went there regularly after that, but I had to wait until that same bouncer was at the door to get in.

In October 1973, I was offered a job as a trainee glass cutter. I accepted because it paid twenty pounds a week and it was a day shift. The company was Milburn and Ellis, a glass cutting and glazing firm. Once I had started this job, I realised it was a mistake as I didn't get along with the owner. After six months, I left.

When I was seventeen years old, I wanted to learn how to drive, so for several weeks I had a driving lesson for two pounds a time. I soon realised that I wouldn't be able to afford to pay for my driving test, so I stopped learning.

My priorities started to change at that age. Socialising was more important, like going to pubs and clubs and on trips to Blackpool for the day, with old friends and new ones. Quite a few of us used to go on those day trips to Blackpool. We would hire a forty-seater bus for the day and set off at eight in the morning, leaving Blackpool at midnight. At the end of the day, a couple of people always missed the bus back home.

Every year, we also attended the Durham Big Meeting, or the Miners' Gala, an event that had been going since 1871, even before my grandad was born. Over the years, it had hosted some of the biggest Labour politicians, and thousands of people turned up.

After the glass cutter job, I worked in a local plastics factory for a month, on a three-shift system. Then, in 1974 I started working on the building sites, which I did for several years. My first job was building a new road bridge across the River Wear in Durham City, for a company called Brims Construction. The pay was a lot more than I had been earning in the past. I negotiated a deal for my board and lodgings with my mam so in the end I earned £32.50 a week, and we halved it so I was getting sixteen pounds. And if I worked overtime, I got more. I started on this job with my cousin Peter Casey and a friend called David Fleming. All of us came from Sherburn Road Estate.

We really enjoyed this job, but we did see a few bad accidents. One day, we had just finished our bait (break) and were heading to the other side of the bridge. We had to walk around the city because the middle section wasn't completed, though. As we came off the site, we heard an awful scream from across the road. We saw an articulated lorry, and under the back wheels, a bloodied head. We thought someone was trapped. I remember our ganger (chargehand) saying, 'Come on, leave that, there's plenty people there to help. Let's get back to work.'

We found out later it was a ten-year-old American tourist, who had been caught in the back wheels of the lorry as it cut the corner. The screaming we heard was the child's mother. They were meant to go home the next morning. A very sad day indeed.

There was another incident, when my cousin Peter saw smoke coming from the roof of the County Hotel next to our job. Within minutes, large flames were leaping up, but the firemen told us to keep working. It took them three hours to get the fire under control.

Later, a press reporter came onto the site to ask us if we had witnessed anything. He walked under an end section of the bridge where it was quite dark, as some of the shuttering was still up. There was an uncovered manhole where my cousin was working and as the reporter walked over to us, talking as he went, he fell right into the manhole. He wasn't badly hurt, but we think his pride was. I know we shouldn't have, but we did have a good laugh. We enjoyed working on this job, learning a lot of building skills.

The year I turned eighteen, my dad got me club cards for the local working men's club. I didn't go there often, though, as I preferred the local pubs. Dad used to say, 'Why do you go into the pubs and nightclubs? It's a lot cheaper in the working mens' club.'

On a Sunday night, my friends and I used to go to Durham City Rugby Club. One time, we were there and I said to this girl, 'Can I walk you to the bus stop?'

'No,' she said, and then paused. 'There are no buses - they're on strike.'

I then asked if I could walk her home and she said yes, and that's how I met my wife, Mandy.

MARRIAGE

Mandy and I have been together ever since, for nearly fifty years now. When we started courting, we saw each other nearly every night. In October 1975, after we had been courting for a year, her mam and dad invited me to go to

Benidorm with their family. I said yes. It was the first time I had been abroad, and so the first time I had flown on an aeroplane. What a time we had! Red hot weather, pubs that were open all day, and no half ten closing time like back home.

That same year, we got engaged and started saving in a joint bank account for a deposit for our first house. We married in March 1977 and moved into our first home; a three-bed terrace in Gilesgate Moor, Durham City. It needed doing up a bit. For our honeymoon, we went to Benidorm for a week. The day we flew out, on 27 March 1977, two passenger planes crashed on the runway at Tenerife. A huge number of people, 583, were killed.

In August 1978, Mandy and I flew to Tenerife for a week's holiday, to celebrate her pregnancy with our first child. As we were starting to land, the man sitting next to me said, 'Look at this on the side of the runway.' When I looked, there was a large heap of wreckage from one of the planes that had crashed there the previous year. It was horrible and put me off flying afterwards. We have flown quite a lot since that day, but every time I get on a plane, I remember what I saw that day, and think of those poor people. God rest their souls.

During our holiday in Tenerife, we went to see a mock bullfight for tourists. At the time, this sort of thing happened all over Spain and its islands. We had been to them before and taken part. At this one, I said to Mandy, 'I'm going to have a go, but I'm not going to have any alcohol before I do it.'

Twelve of us volunteered, and were given red capes. Once you were in the ring, a young bull was released, and you had to be a bit like a matador for as long as your nerves would let you. I was last in the queue, and watched all these daft lads in the ring. The bulls were about four and a half feet tall, and a bit frisky. There were two thousand people watching and laughing at us.

I was last to go. I stood in the centre of the ring with my cape, waiting. Then they released the bull. It was at least five-feet tall, and full of life. I shouted at it and shook my cape. It ran at me. I held my cape to one side as I had been told. Then, bang! It came straight at me instead and I went flying. I hit the ground and the bull ran to the other end of the ring. My adrenalin was really pumping!

I thought that this probably wouldn't happen again, so I rushed to my feet and got the bull's attention. Again, it came charging at me. As I stepped to one side, the bull followed and bang, I was on my backside again!

I was determined to not let it get me a third time. Standing up, I shouted again, and the bull came charging towards me. I took a large step to one side, waving the cape, and bang, it hit me yet again! This time it kept still and came in to get me with its horns. I ran like the wind to get out of the ring safely.

Afterwards, we had a good laugh, and the people gave me a good cheer. I needed a few drinks to calm down, and I had a big bruise from my chin to my chest. A couple of years later, the Spanish government stopped those mock bullfights for tourists, for health and safety reasons.

Our eldest child Benjamin was born on 26 October 1978. Mandy and I were very proud, but also a little bit anxious about the new responsibility. We had to make sure we were doing the right thing for three people now, instead of just the two of us.

WORK

Back at home, I now worked for a specialist masonry company called, J & W Lowry's. For eighteen months, I renovated Durham Cathedral's bell tower. We took the nineteenth-century wooden bell tower out and replaced it with a steel structure. They dropped the bells and sent them away to London for a peal, which meant the muck from the centuries was scraped off, possibly with acid, and the bells were given the tone they'd had originally.

The bell tower had been put together with 24-inch oak beams, held in place with wooden pegs. When we took it apart, I kept the pegs and I used to give them to tourists as I was walking round the cathedral. I cut one of the old beams into a two-inch slice which showed the joints at the end, and gave it to my mother-in-law. She had it on her hearth for years.

This was one of the hardest jobs I ever did as a labourer, as I was feeding to six stonemasons. I had to mix the sand, cement and gravel on four boards and send it up the tower for them to work with. At first, we had to carry it up, and then we used a straightforward pulley and a bucket.

There was no electricity involved until we finally got a small electric hoist and a cage. We needed a radio to tell them at the top when to drop it down to us, 200 feet at the bottom of the tower. We were inside the cathedral though, and sometimes there were people below. One time, we had to make them stop halfway because there was a Mass being taken underneath by Bishop Runcie.

When we were rebuilding, the stonemasons wrote our names on a piece of paper and put it inside a glass bottle to bury in the stonework on the tower.

After this I worked on Pittington Church, putting concrete stitches around the tower because it was wind damaged and was pulling apart. At Shincliffe Church, they'd had a fire and some of the windows had blown out and the pointing had gone. I loved being with this firm and I got to work on some of the oldest churches in Durham, which was fascinating.

I then decided to leave the building work for a while and went to work at a local meat factory as a dispatch operative. I was promoted several times as an area leading chargehand.

After about a year at the meat factory, I decided I wanted to better myself for my family, so I resigned and enrolled on a management course at the local college. This was a poor decision as I struggled with the written work, but I managed to gain a management certificate. After finishing the course, I found myself without a job and unable to get one for a few months.

Eventually, I got a job in a large local warehouse for the VG shops as a warehouseman/forklift driver. This job had the benefit that you could buy any damaged goods very cheaply. When my son started eating solids, I used to buy bashed tins of baby food at a fraction of the cost in the shops.

A year later, along with my friend Barry, I started working for Durham City Council in the parks department. We cut grass in the local villages around the city. I stayed in this job for about a year.

But then my wife and I decided that we needed to cut our costs, so we decided to sell our home and moved to Ferryhill village, eight miles outside the city, in County Durham. There they were selling old miners' houses cheap, and with the money we got from our house in Durham, we bought one. We could modernise it and still have money left in the bank.

While living in Ferryhill, I went on a six-month training course in bricklaying. I got a job as a jobbing bricklayer a few times, then with two lads from Ferryhill went into a two-and-one squad (two bricklayers and a labourer). We worked together for a few years and moved on.

FAMILY

Our life in Ferryhill was good. We made lots of friends, and I was involved with Ferryhill Celtic Football Club. I used to drink in the big club.

On 13 April 1982, our second son Matthew was born. At the time, we didn't know that our family already had a connection to the house. I only realised this once my interest in family history developed. In 2010, I found some of my dad's cousins who, at that time, lived in Ilkley, West Yorkshire; their mam was my grandad's sister. They told me that they had been born in, and lived in, Ferryhill for a while before their family moved. They said that they had lived on Davy Street. This was my road. When I told them that my wife and I lived at 62 Davy Street, they said, 'That's where my twin sister and me were born on 13 April 1926.' I told them our second son, Matthew, had also been born there, on 13 April 1982! We all thought it was amazing.

During our children's childhoods, in the summer, we went on holidays to Butlins, Blackpool, Spain, Majorca, and in the late 80s, Centre Parcs. I think the last holiday we had together was when our oldest son was sixteen years old, just before he finished school. We went to Palma Nova, Majorca, for a week. After that, the boys didn't think it was cool going on holiday with their parents.

After about five years living in Ferryhill, we decided it was time to move back to Durham City. We sold our house, and moved to Carrville, about two miles outside the city centre. We put a large cash deposit down, but we still needed a mortgage.

At that time, I was working as a bricklayer on an extension to Belmont Comprehensive School. The foreman came over and said, 'Your wife has been on the phone. She dropped something on her foot and wants you to go home.'

Turns out, she had dropped the pasting table. Her foot had swelled up like a balloon and she had it in a bowl of cold water. I needed to take her to the hospital. While helping her to the car, our two- and six-year-old sons were in the house, throwing water at each other from the bowl. I got them into the car as well and we all went to the hospital. We discovered that Mandy had burst the blood vessels in her foot. It was put in a plaster, and she was given crutches for six weeks.

When we got back home, we took two steps to get through the door, and I went to lift Mandy. Snap! My back went and I dropped her. With the help of our sons, we struggled to get into the house. I had to phone the doctor to come out. When she arrived, she said, 'You'll have to go to the hospital.' Again.

The doctor phoned for an ambulance to take me in. While waiting to see a doctor at the hospital, a nurse was talking to me. 'We have just had two people earlier today with the same surname,' she said. I told her that I knew one was my wife, and the other was my niece, Joanna, who'd broken her arm.

The doctor sent me for an x-ray and said I would be kept in hospital for a week. I had to be put in traction as I had torn all the muscles in my back. That was on a Thursday, and at the weekend the Band Aid concert was on TV. I spent a week in the hospital, and Mandy had her plaster on for four weeks. It wasn't funny at the time, but when we look back now, we have a good laugh about it.

Then the building work dried up. I knew that I needed to find steadier and more permanent work, so I got a job at Mono Containers, the local plastics factory. I had worked there for a month when I was eighteen, but this time the job was for a forklift driver/warehouseman, on a three-shift system, Monday to Friday.

After about five years, I moved into the factory as a machine operator on a three-month temporary contract in the warehouse. I got on well with all the lads so when I came to the end of my contract, the lads thought I should be put on a permanent contract. The management, however, said they wouldn't do this. So then the lads told the management that we were not going to work overtime unless they gave me a permanent contract. In the end, I was given the contract.

I then became a union shop steward for several years, helping others with their employment problems and negotiating pay rises etc. I was there for about ten years until I was made redundant in 1995.

COLLEGE
While working at this job, I was struggling to help my sons with their schoolwork, so I enrolled at the local college

in the Adult Learning Centre. I was introduced to my tutor, Jo Colley, who asked me to write about myself. I wrote about two hundred words. I don't know how long it took me, but I thought it was loads.

Jo encouraged me and over the next few months, she gave me the confidence to enrol at the University of Durham on some short management courses. As I completed each twelve-week-long course, Jo would encourage me to do another. After completing three, Jo said I should try the twelve-month-long Human Resource Management course, which included eight two-thousand-word assignments, and a ten-thousand-word assignment at the end. With Jo's help and Mandy's support, I did all these courses and achieved an average mark of 57%. I was really proud of myself.

Jo nominated me for the North East Adult Learner of the Year Award in 1997, which I won! Looking back to when I was writing those first two hundred words, and thinking about finishing three years later with ten-thousand words, I know what an achievement I had accomplished.

While on these courses, I was made redundant from my job in the plastics factory. So, in 1995, I began working at the University of Durham, in the security department as a community liaison officer. I dealt with students and problems in the local community, such as parties, parking and peace-keeping. I really enjoyed it, even though I'd had no formal training.

My partner, Keith, and I would start work at six at night and finish at four the next morning. We would wait for phone calls with complaints about student behaviour in and around the city. Some were about noisy parties going on into the early hours. We would go to the address, and, over and over, the excuses would be the same: it was someone's birthday; they didn't think it was too loud; the neighbours knew they were having a party. We usually resolved the problem without involving the police.

Another regular complaint was about students blocking in other vehicles. Our way of resolving this was to go to the street and block in the student's cars then wait for them to come back.

'Could you move your vehicle?' they'd ask. 'I've got somewhere to be.'

We would say, 'Just like your neighbours trying to get to work. You and your fellow students need to stop blocking them in. We'll be back every night until you all get the message.' The problem would normally be resolved after that.

HEALTH

I have always liked keeping fit, whether it was running, swimming or circuit training. In 1998, I even took up boxing training. I started this when our youngest son Matthew was going to the boxing club. I used to drop him off and wait until he was finished to take him home, but then I decided I might as well join in too. I trained for about a year and felt the fittest I had ever been.

One day while at the local working man's club, a young lad said that he wanted a sparring partner. Foolishly, I thought that I was fit enough, so I volunteered. He and I went to my friend's house, who had a boxing set-up in his garage. The lad was a lot younger than me and was really fit.

We started sparring and in round one, the lad got under my guard and hit me in the ribs. It really hurt, but I didn't want to show it. This happened four times in that round. Halfway through the second, I was hit another two times in the ribs. I had to stop because I couldn't breathe.

The next day I couldn't bear the pain and went to hospital. I was x-rayed and the doctor said that I had a broken rib. He gave me some painkillers and told me to come back if it got worse.

Three days later, while at work, the pain became unbearable, and I went back to the hospital at four in the morning. I was taken into intensive care after they x-rayed me. Most of the ribs on my right side were broken, and I was in danger of rupturing my spleen.

I spent two days in intensive care, two days on a ward, and then I was let home. I laugh about it now, but the pain was awful. I have never volunteered for anything like that again. Another lesson learnt!

After about eight years working at the university, our department was restructured and I was appointed as a security supervisor. In 2011, I left this job because of health problems, and have never had another job since.

TRAVEL

After our children no longer wanted to go on holiday with us, Mandy and I started going to different places, outside Europe. The first place we went to was Las Vegas, for our twenty-fifth wedding anniversary in 2002, to renew our wedding vows. We thought it was a great experience. The most memorable thing was the Grand Canyon, which was breathtaking!

In the next two years, we flew to Jamaica and Cuba and learned about the local culture. We learned scuba-diving and I got my open-water scuba diving certificate in Cuba, where we also swam with dolphins and rode on their backs, all experiences we will never forget.

Our friends, Billy and Dawn Pallister, had emigrated to Australia in 1978. When they came back to England, in 1982, they lived on the same street as us in Ferryhill, where their daughter Alana was born. They couldn't settle here, however, so they moved back to Australia in 1984 when Alana was six weeks old. It was a dream of ours to visit them.

In 2005 Matthew, our youngest son, married Catherine in Durham City. They had their first child, Ayla Malia, in 2006. Our first grandchild. My new granddaughter really changed me. At least once a week, she would stop over at our house while Mandy went to work. At first, it was daunting, not knowing the right things to do.

I then asked Ayla's mam and dad to write out her routine so I could stick to it. I took Ayla all over, to local parks and to swimming lessons for babies and toddlers, showing her off to my family and friends. I drove Mandy mad when she got home from work, telling her about my day with Ayla: her first smile, sitting up for the first time, starting to crawl and walking.

I realised then that Mandy had seen all these things with our sons when they grew up. I had missed them, however, since I was always at work or out for a drink on weekends. I regret missing out on some of those experiences with my own two children.

The same year, our eldest son Benjamin married Sarah on the island of Crete. By February 2008, both our daughters-in-law were expecting babies and they were born within six days of each other. The first born was Matthew and Catherine's second daughter, Eden, in Durham City. On 24 February, Ben and Sarah's first daughter, Caitlyn, was born in Northampton. Both Ayla and Eden stayed with us once a week. Mandy was not working at this time, so we looked after the children together. On some weekends, we went down to Northampton and stayed overnight, to give Ben and Sarah a bit of a break, because Caitlyn was poorly for the first few months after she was born.

We achieved our dream in 2010 and went to Australia. We stayed with Billy and Dawn in Melbourne for five nights, and went on to Cairns and Brisbane, finishing off in Sydney. What an experience! What a country! The history of the people over the last three hundred years was amazing as it's such a short space of time to build the country like it is today. The natural history is wonderful: the coast, the rain forests and the wildlife, some of which can be found nowhere else in the world. You could get close up to snakes, crocs and sharks, and there were parrots, budgies and other exotic birds just flying around.

We stayed in Singapore for one night on the flights there and back, and of course went to the famous Raffles Hotel for a drink. When we were walking back to our own hotel, I noticed a $10 note on the ground. As we continued walking, we found even more cash. It came to $120 in total! Then my wife noticed that her bag had a split at the bottom, and it was her own money I'd been picking up. We had a good laugh about that!

Billy and Dawn still live in Australia and have two grown-up daughters now; their second child, Stevie, was born in Australia. The last time we went there, we stayed in Sydney and Dawn and Billy visited us for five days. We had a great time together. We went to Uluru (Ayres Rock) for four days and finished in Port Douglas, Tropical North Queensland.

MORE GRANDCHILDREN

In February 2011, Ben and Sarah's second daughter, and our fourth granddaughter, Lauren, was born in Northampton. We went over there at least three times a year to see them, and they would come up to Durham to see Mandy and me and the rest of the family.

In September 2011, Matthew and Catherine's third daughter, and our fifth granddaughter, Miley, was born in Durham City. She was poorly, in and out of hospital for the first year of her life, but once her medication was sorted, she was fine.

It was at this time that Ayla, our oldest granddaughter, started doing karate at a local club. She used to get upset when she first joined, and I asked if she wanted me to do it with her. She said yes, so I did. Our granddaughter Eden joined when she was old enough.

The girls lasted two years, but I continued doing karate for five years. Towards the end of my time, I was doing some light touch sparring when I got a knee to my ribs. I knew something had broken, but I continued a bit more. I then got another knee to the ribs, and stopped. The pain wasn't too bad, so I went home. There, I sneezed, and that was when the pain became unbearable. Mandy took me to the hospital and the doctors had me x-rayed. I had four broken ribs! They kept me in hospital for a week. I had not learned my lesson last time, when I broke my ribs by boxing, but at nearly sixty years old, I had well and truly learned it now.

We continued looking after our three granddaughters from Durham at least once a week, until Matthew and Catherine separated in 2016. Ayla, Eden and Miley continued to stop over for one night a week at our house, and at odd times call to see us. We enjoyed it when all five of our grandchildren stayed with us. We used to take them to local beaches, like Seaham Harbour, Crimdon Dene and Tynemouth Beach.

We also took them to the open-air museum at Beamish, which has a Victorian school; old houses; trams and old buses to ride on; a drift mine you can go down; and all sorts of workings to do with the pit. We would spend the whole day there, telling them, 'This was how our grandparents used to live. Even when we were children, some of the houses were still like they are at Beamish.' We never wanted to go home because we had all enjoyed it so much.

While we were at Beamish with our grandchildren, I used to think about my grandparents, as they were born in these times. I can't remember my grandad Malia much as I was only four when he died in 1960. But I'll never forget when he laid out in a coffin at home, and we had to go down and see him. Someone lifted me up to give him a kiss. That was sixty-one years ago, and the memory is still with me. It is not a bad or frightening memory; this was just what people did then.

My granny Malia died aged eighty-five in 1973. My best

memory of her was that every Saturday afternoon all of her grandchildren came to her house to watch wrestling on the TV. She would cook sausages for all of us in the oven in the fireplace, and I can still taste them now. They were delicious.

My grandad Casey died aged sixty-eight in 1967, and I remember him being funny and dry-humoured. Sometimes he would say, 'Have some sweets, but don't tell your mam. She'll go crackers with me.'

My granny Casey died aged eighty-two in 1982. She was born in County Rosscommon, Ireland, but her mam sadly died when she was a baby. She used to tell me stories about living in Ireland and being brought up by the nuns in Dublin. The story that stuck in her mind was how the nuns would take them to Mass on a Sunday. 'We would have to walk along the cobbled streets on the banks of the River Liffey in our bare feet.'

When I was in my late teens and early years of my marriage, I went to see my gran with my wife and our son Ben. My granny Casey used to call her front room the 'parlour' and when the local priest called to see her, she would ask him in there for a cup of tea. Around eighty years old, she had an operation to remove the bottom part of one of her legs. She had a false leg fitted and one day she started scratching it.

I said, 'That's your false leg you're scratching, Gran.'

'It's my toes,' she replied. 'They feel itchy.' She told us that if she scratched the end of where her leg had been, she got relief from it. She always used to tell me when I would twist on about people to her, 'Our John, it's nice to be nice. It costs nothing to be nice.' She was right, and I say the same thing to my grandchildren today.

As I come to the end of my story, it makes me think about how life goes on, but continues to improve and develop. What is 'normal' will keep changing, for the better. Thinking back to the time when my grandad was born, there were no telephones, no school, not much travel and two world wars. Even in my parents' time, they had to go through a world war, leave school at fourteen, and most things were on ration.

And then there was my time. The street I was born on had forty houses in it. Over the road were three family-run shops selling groceries and cigarettes. You could buy things and pay at the end of the week. The shops had very little choice and if you needed electrical items you had to travel. There was a butcher, one betting shop, three pubs, a large football pitch where a local team played, and a field with pigs in it. We left school at fifteen, and holidays were a local bus to the beach for the day.

In our son's day, children left school at sixteen; TV still closed down at night, and there were limited channels. However, people had more foreign holidays, they owned more cars, and they had more landline phones in their homes.

Now all of that is gone. Local shops have been replaced by shopping complexes and superstores where you can buy almost anything. It's not until you get more mature and start looking back that you can see all the changes that have improved life over the years.

Then I think about my grandchildren's time, and see how even more has changed. What have they got? Plenty more opportunities for going to university; foreign holidays; phones they carry around in their pockets; internet; fast food; shops with everything in them; and everything else that goes with modern-day life. I just wonder, when our grandchildren become grandparents, what will 'normal' be like then? Maybe holidays will be on the moon, or planets even further away. Some of us could even be living in space!

Our family in the back garden of Goodyear Crescent in 1960. My father holding me, and Mam holding my baby sister Denise. Standing are Bridget, Bernadette, Joseph Patrick and Theresa

Me and my dog Dutch, in our back garden, around 1963

Me on my neighbour's motorbike, around 1964

My house group in my first year at St Leonard's, 1967. Front row, third from left, my sister Bernadette. Back row, last on right, myself

The decimal currency calculator issued to everyone

Durham ice rink and MacKay's carpet factory where I first started work

My first building site at New Elvet Bridge in Durham City

Myself at Blackpool with the lads in 1973. Second from left in the group of four at top right

Mandy and I got married on 26 March 1977

You are my golden hour,
My sunlit sea,
My skylark singing
Wild and free . . .

You are my starlight
In indigo dark,
In sad, dying embers,
The shimmering spark;

You are my eagle,
My gentle white dove,
My land bright with springtime . .
You are my love.

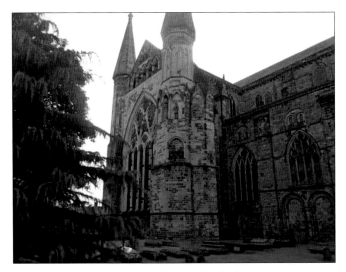

Durham Cathedral

My dad and mam in the 1980s with one of their pigeons, Limpy

Not Just Our Mam

When you were born, you became
A daughter to your mam and dad,
A granddaughter to your grandparents,
A niece to your aunts and uncles,
A sister to your brothers and sisters.

When you were growing up, you became
A friend to the people you knew around the doors and at school,
A work mate when you left school,
A girlfriend to our dad, and then fiancée.

When you married our dad, you became
A wife to our dad,
A daughter-in-law to our grandparents,
A sister-in-law to our aunts and uncles,
An aunty to your brothers and sisters' brother,
And sister-in-laws children,
A mother to all of us six.

When we were growing up, you became
A nurse when we were poorly,
A mother-in-law to our wives and husbands,
A nanna to our children,
A great-nanna to our children's children.

After all of these things you have been in your life,
We understand you have got tired and want to go to sleep.
We don't want to let you go because we love you and you're our mam,
But we know you have to.

So, one last goodnight and God bless.
Sleep in peace 'Our Mam', we love you.
xxxxxx

Poem by the author, John Malia, written in 2018 just after the death
of his mother, Bridget Malia

Matthew and Ben on holiday at Centre Parcs in Sherwood Forest

Matthew and Ben's school photo when they were at Belmont
Infant and Juniors

The four of us at Mandy's brother's wedding

Four generations of Malias: my mam, me, our two sons, and our three oldest grandchildren, 2008

Visting our friends, Dawn and Billy Pallister, in Australia, 2010

Me, Mandy and Big Frank at the Metro Centre, Gateshead in about 2018

Mandy and I with our five granddaughters, 2016

*Our lovely granddaughters in 2019. Back row,
Ayla. Middle row, Caitlyn and Eden. Front row,
Miley and Lauren*